To Rejoice Is a Choice

CREDITS
Project Manager: Dr. Bob Marshall
Assistant: Rochelle Chalifoux
Transcription: Cyndilu Marshall
Page Design and Layout: Linda Stubblefield
Proofreading: Debbie Borsh, Elaine Colsten, Martha Gilbert

To order additional books by Dr. Jack Schaap,
please contact:
HYLES PUBLICATIONS
523 Sibley Street • Hammond, Indiana 46320
www.hylespublications.com
e-mail: info@hylespublications.com

To Rejoice is a Choice

Dr. Jack Schaap

*T*hank you to my editorial advisor, Mrs. Linda Stubblefield, who has labored for many hours to make my thoughts and heart clear to the reader. Upon her graduation from Hyles-Anderson College in 1977, Linda began working for Marlene Evans with Christian Womanhood. After working in various capacities, she now serves as the assistant editor of the Christian Womanhood magazine. She is married to David Stubblefield, the academic dean at Hyles-Anderson College. The Stubblefields are the parents of two adult daughters.

Dedication

For many families, life has seemed extraordinarily unkind. Circumstances have confined or diminished the quality of life they might have enjoyed. I have chosen the following families to represent the many millions of those who are forced by circumstances to either turn a deep shade of bitter or to make the choice to rejoice. The following families in First Baptist Church of Hammond have one of their members who has been unexpectedly confined to a wheelchair. They have also chosen to rejoice.

The Comstock Family

Nicholas Comstock was born with the CMV Virus. That virus along with twin transfusion problems left him in a wheelchair from birth. He is considered to have a form of cerebral palsy now. Nicholas is 16 years old.

Bill and Cricket Boyd

Bill Boyd was pastor of Freedom Baptist Church in Virginia in February 1999. He had been working a side job on a construction site when he was loading up tools to go home. He fell 30 feet onto the sidewalk below. The accident left him a quadriplegic.

Randy and Tina Rodgers

On September 11, 1995, Randy Rodgers was painting the trim on the highest point of a house when he overextended his reach and fell. The accident left him a quadriplegic C- 67. Randy and Tina have three children.

The Depper Family
David Depper was diagnosed at 11 months of age with cerebral palsy. David is 23 years old.

Will and Karen Hinson
On October 13, 2003, Will was involved in a horrible car accident. He suffered a fracture to his C2-C3 vertebrae that left him a quadriplegic.

Karen Ferguson
Karen was born with badly deformed legs. Doctors told her she would be more mobile without her legs than with them, so she had her legs removed very early in life. Karen has come to First Baptist Church for over 20 years, and she still struggles with the complications of her lifelong spina bifida.

Paul Miller
Paul was diagnosed with multiple sclerosis at the age of 13. He is now a student at Hyles-Anderson College.

Jose Delgado
Jose was born with spina bifida and has never been able to walk. He graduated from City Baptist High School and now attends Hyles-Anderson College. Jose is 20 years of age.

Contents

Carpe diem![1]
Rejoice while you are alive; enjoy the day;
live life to the fullest; make the most of what
you have. It is later than you think.
                                        –Horace

Introduction

Many of the sermons I preach or the books I write are the direct result of counseling with multitudes of people. First Baptist Church of Hammond is a microcosm of the world around me. If my people are struggling in certain areas, I can be certain that many others are also dealing with the same issues. I have been and still am particularly concerned with depression, clinical depression, mood disorders, and the other "buzz" words for the sadness which seems to creep into our lives—even into the lives of excellent Christians. Depression, which is the Bible word *heaviness*, is a widespread problem invading our homes and churches.

Depression is one of the most common mental disorders and affects up to 25 percent of women and 10 percent of men. About one in nine Americans will experience a depressive episode in a given year.[2]

The Diagnostic and Statistical Manual of Mental Disorders, Fourth Edition Text Revision (DSM-IV-TR) lists the following criteria for major depressive episode:

Five or more of the following symptoms have been present during the same two-week period and represent a change from previous functioning; at least one of the symptoms is either (1) depressed mood or (2) loss of interest or pleasure.

• Depressed mood most of the day, nearly every day, as

indicated by either subjective report (e.g. feels sad or empty) or observation by others (e.g., appears tearful).

- Markedly diminished interest or pleasure in all, or almost all, activities most of the day, nearly every day (as indicated by either subjective account or observation made by others)
- Significant weight loss when not dieting or weight gain (e.g., a change of more than 5 percent of body weight in a month), or decrease or increase in appetite nearly every day
- Insomnia or hypersomnia [excessive sleep] nearly every day
- Psychomotor agitation or retardation [slowing down] nearly every day (observable by others, not merely subjective feelings of restlessness or being slowed down)
- Fatigue or loss of energy nearly every day
- Feelings of worthlessness or of excessive or inappropriate guilt (which may be delusional) nearly every day (not merely self-reproach or guilt about being sick)
- Diminished ability to think or concentrate, or indecisiveness, nearly every day (either by subjective account or as observed by others)
- Recurrent thoughts of death (not just fear of dying), recurrent suicidal ideation [thinking] without a specific plan, a suicide attempt, or a specific plan for committing suicide[3]

The DSM-IV-TR is *the* recognized book in the medical and forensic world to consult for mental disorders and issues. The purpose of the DSM-IV-TR is to provide clear descriptions of diagnostic categories in order to enable clinicians and investigators to diagnose, communicate about, study, and treat people. The proper use of these criteria requires specialized training that provides both a body of knowledge and clinical skills.[4]

Medical doctors, psychologists, and psychiatrists prescribe drugs, talk therapy, light therapy, music therapy, and try many other methods and means to combat the pervasiveness of depression.

Depression may result from psychosocial problems such as marital conflict or loss of a significant relationship, or job, occupational, or economic instability. Usually a combination of biological, psychological, and environmental factors that contribute to an episode of depression.[5]

The issue of depression must be addressed in our Christian circles. "Depression may affect as many as one in eight teenagers. In all, it affects more than 17 million Americans each year. Depression is about twice as common in women as it is in men. This gender difference begins during the teen years."[6]

"Depression affects an estimated 18 million Americans each year—more people than cancer and almost as many people as heart disease."[7]

The cost of depression to American business is staggering:
$7.5 billion — loss of earnings due to suicide
$12.4 billion — cost of treatment and rehabilitation
$23.8 billion — cost of absenteeism and lost productivity
Final ticket price: Taken together, depression costs society and the business community more than $43.7 billion each year.[8]

America needs help! *"I will lift up mine eyes unto the hills, from whence cometh my help. My help cometh from the LORD, which made heaven and earth."* (Psalm 121:1, 2)

Several non-medical approaches have been found to be helpful in the treatment of depression:
A. A central feature of major depression is sleep disturbance. Anyone with a few nights of poor quality sleep will notice four common problems: increased emotional sensitivity, irritability, daytime fatigue, and difficulty concentrating.

B. Regular exercise is one the most important and powerful things you can do to decrease depression. Regular exercise has been associated with increases of certain brain chemicals—endorphins and serotonin—both of which can reduce depressive symptoms.

C. One decisive action you can take during times of depression is to reduce or eliminate caffeine. This widely used drug is found in coffee, tea, soft drink and chocolate, and hides in a number of pain medications and diet pills.

D. Diet and health are related. A high blood-fat level alone can cause depression, and reducing fat intake can markedly improve depressive symptoms. A severe Vitamin B deficiency (e.g. thiamine, folic acid, niacin) can disturb brain function and lead to high levels of anxiety and depression. Folic acid supplements have produced dramatic relief of symptoms of depression. A regular diet rich in omega-3 fatty acids has been shown to reduce intense mood instability. Dr. Barbara Strupp, associate professor of psychology at Cornell University, confirms: the best way to get the right combination of necessary brain nutrients and depression-fighting neurochemicals is to eat a balanced diet.[9]

Sleep is the time for your body, emotions, brain, and mind to restore themselves to proper functioning. Sleep is the guardian of health.[10]

Certainly there is merit to all of these ways to battle depression. I sincerely believe the heaviness that suddenly enters the life of a Christian can be combated with mega-doses of reading and memorizing the Book, listening to sound preaching, praying, fellowshipping with fellow Christians, being thankful, getting busy, and making a conscious choice to choose happiness instead of sadness. To that end I have written, Rejoice Is a Choice.

"When you were born, you cried, and the world rejoiced! Live your life so that when you die, the world cries, and you rejoice!"
    –Unknown

1

To Rejoice Is a Choice

Suggested Reading:
Philippians 4:1-13

Rejoicing is your choice. In Philippians 4:4 the Bible commands us, *"Rejoice in the Lord alway: and again I say, Rejoice."* A person chooses whether or not he wants to be full of joy. He chooses whether he doesn't want to have joy.

Personally, I don't understand gloomy Christians, and I don't think I ever will. As a matter of fact, I really don't ever want to understand gloomy Christians. A lot of people offer excuses for their gloominess and say, "You don't know what I am going through." I thank God because I would not want to look the way or act the way most gloomy Christians look and act!

> "You can complain because roses have thorns, or you can rejoice because thorns have roses."
> –Tom Wilson
> (creator of Ziggy)

Thankfully, I was taught by a great man for nearly a quarter of a century that a Christian chooses whether or not to be joyful. That man was my father-in-law, Dr. Jack Hyles, who chose to be an upbeat, positive, happy-spirited Christian. He had every right to be a gloomy, downcast, downhearted, unhappy, miserable wretch of a Christian, but he lived a joyful life.

I can mentally understand the human logic behind a person's

being gloomy. When I hear the reasons why a person is sad or downhearted, I believe I can understand the reasoning. Humanly, I understand the person's choice of words. His words make an impression in my mind, my mind sends an acknowledging signal, and my mental capacity is sufficient to understand his mental reasoning as to why he is downhearted and gloomy. My problem is that I just don't agree with him!

Of course, everyone experiences a bad day occasionally. I am addressing those with the long-term unhappy, gloomy, "I-wish-I-wasn't-saved," "I-am-so-miserable," "I-don't-know-why-God-doesn't-change-my-life" kind of attitude. I cannot help but think of certain members of First Baptist Church of Hammond, Indiana, who could easily have that gloomy attitude. At this writing, one of our excellent church families just buried one of their loved ones. After the graveside service at our Memory Lane Cemetery, we had a time of remembrance. I marveled at the family talking and laughing together. Certainly, none of us were happy because a husband/father/grandfather was gone; rather, we were reminiscing and reliving some wonderful memories.

One of the grandkids shared, "Grandpa always knew how to get us grandkids with him. He would buy us a Dairy Queen treat and pizza." The family laughed together and enjoyed that memory. They shared wonderful memories of sitting and talking around the dinner table.

Not long after that funeral, one of the sons, who is on our deacon board, met me, hugged me, and said, "I just want to thank you for preaching my father's funeral." He had a smile on his face. As I watched him walk away, I thought, "Rejoicing is a choice." We choose whether to be gloomy, miserable, unhappy, unkempt, downhearted, and down in the dumps.

The same excuse is paramount in the life of a non-rejoicing person. I tire of hearing that same old excuse, "You just don't know what I am going through."

"Yes, I believe I do know; and on the other side, no one knows what I go through. However, I choose not to share my problems because I don't want to have a pity party!"

I am reminded of my sister's work in needlepoint. With thread, needle, and canvass, Kristi creates beautiful pictures accented with epigrammatic statements. Through the years she has filled her house with her beautiful work, and she has graciously shared her work with us. One of my favorites is one that is displayed in her house. That stitched picture depicts a clothesline stretched between two poles, and different articles of clothing are clothespinned to the line. The motto reads, "If all our problems were hung on a line, you would take yours, and I would take mine."

"There are joys which long to be ours. God sends ten thousand truths which come about us like birds seeking inlet; but we are shut up to them, and so they bring us nothing, but sit and sing a while upon the roof, and then fly away."
–Henry Ward Beecher

If I could display all my problems in front of you and you could display all your problems in front of me, I can guarantee you that you would walk away and say, "Thank God, I have mine and not his!" In turn, I have no doubt that I would walk away from yours saying, "Thank God, I have mine and not yours!" I have yet to meet anyone who wanted to swap problems with another. In the same way, choosing to rejoice is also your choice.

I was given a *Newsweek* magazine that detailed some startling facts about teenage depression. On the table of contents page, teen depression is listed as the cover story with the following press release: "Three million teenagers struggle with depression. As groundbreaking brain research shows why adolescents may be particularly vulnerable, teens, their parents and their schools are wrestling with how to tell the difference between what's 'just a phase' and what might be more serious."[1]

"Some researchers think that the stress of a high divorce rate, rising academic expectations, and social pressure may be pushing more kids over the edge....Depressed adolescents are at high risk for school failure, social isolation, promiscuity, "self-medication" with drugs or alcohol, and suicide—now the third leading cause of death among 10- to 24-year-olds."[2]

Researchers and doctors are desperately seeking treatments for depression. "The NIMH [National Institutes of Mental Health] recently launched a major 12-city initiative called the Treatment for Adolescents With Depression Study to help determine which regimens—Prozac, talk therapy or some combination—work best on 12- to 18-year-olds."[3] Another NIMH study is being conducted to look at some newer medications like Effexor and Paxil which may help adolescents whose depression has become resistant to Prozac. "On college campuses, experts say cases of depression are too often misdiagnosed as mononucleosis or chronic-fatigue syndrome."[4]

A 17-year-old from St. Paul, Minnesota, "has suffered from depression since he was 8, but school officials first thought he had attention deficit disorder. It took more than two years to figure a good treatment for this boy. Desipramine, one of the older antidepressants, didn't work....A month ago he switched to a once-a-day drug called Celexa and says he is doing better. He even managed to get through breaking up with his long-term girlfriend without missing a day of school."[5]

Depression is the most common of all the psychiatric disorders. Each year, more than 100 million people worldwide develop clinically recognizable depression. Depression has a significant personal cost: As many as 15% of individuals with severe recurrent depression attempt to commit suicide.[6]

A study at Duke University says "there is already evidence from other studies supporting short-term behavioral therapy and drugs like Prozac and Paxil. But that regimen works only in about 60 percent of the cases, and almost half of those patients relapse within a year of stopping treatment."[7] "A recent report from the Centers of Disease Control found that 19 percent of high-school students had suicidal thoughts, and more than 2 million of them actually began planning to take their own lives."[8]

One of those interviewed said in 1999 during her junior year at a New York City high school, "I was obsessed with death. I talked about it with everyone." [I wonder to what music she was listening.] "With her parents' help though, she found a therapist just before the start of her senior year 'who put a name to what I'd been feeling.' My therapist made me realize it, face it, and get over it." She also received a prescription for Prozac. Although she had some hesitations about Prozac, "It really did help me," she says. "So did the talk therapy. The first part of the healing process... was becoming more self-aware. They taught me to get some perspective."[9]

"Researchers are only beginning to understand its [serotonin's] complex role in the functioning of the body and brain—and how doctors can make adjustments when the chemical's levels go out of balance. So far, the tools [like Prozac] used to manipulate serotonin in the brain are more like machetes than they are like scalpels—crudely effective, but capable of doing plenty of collateral damage."[10]

"The main problem areas with which most depressed people deal are feelings of low self-esteem, aggression against the self, feelings of grief and loss, feelings of anger and disappointment, feelings of deception in a relationship, unmet dependency needs, and denial of hidden rage."[11]

Drugs and talk, drugs and talk—the world believes that drugs and talk regimens can cure depression. I am not a medical doctor, nor am I an expert in any field of medicine. However, I can read materials written by doctors and medical experts to grasp an understanding of a particular problem. I believe that God gives doctors great wisdom and discernment, and the world is certainly a better place for having doctors. Sometimes God chooses to work through the knowledge of a wise medical doctor. God's goodness comes in many forms, and we must surely include the medical world. However, I do strongly recommend that a person not limit himself to what one doctor says. It is always wise to seek a second opinion. When a doctor says, "Fill this prescription," know about the medication. Read the package inserts!

In over 40 references,[12] the Bible says, *"Take heed to thyself,"* or *"Take heed, and hearken,"* or *"children take heed,"* or *"take heed unto thyself."* In Psalm 39:1, David said, *"…I will take heed to my ways…."* Obviously God wanted the Christian to pay particular attention to himself and be cognizant of what makes him tick.

The renowned philosopher Socrates said, "Know thyself." Knowing yourself means studying yourself. If you have been diagnosed with a chronic illness, be a good student and research everything you can about your illness. Read what reputable sources, such as Mayo Clinic, have available. Do your homework! Just because we have a high school diploma or a college degree hanging on the wall does not mean that learning stops!

I guarantee I may not know or understand with what problem an individual is struggling, but I know beyond a doubt that God does! Sad to say, some wonderful Christians have taken the Word of God and placed big parentheses around certain passages and said, "Except for me." "This works," they say, "except for me."

Reading the Bible and meditating on His Word is the best antidepressant mankind has! However, these depressed Christians erroneously believe they have tried God's "spiritual Prozac" or "spiritual Paxil," and they give up and just say, "God doesn't work; His methods do not work for me." They have never learned that rejoicing is a choice.

A prescription is given for depression in Philippians 4:1-13. God calls our attention to several statements about how we get out of the gloomy "blues."

1. Depression is a result of unreconciled differences between people. In Philippians 4:2 Paul speaks of two women who were not getting along very well. *"I beseech Euodias, and* *beseech Syntyche, that they be of the same mind in the Lord.*" One of the major reasons for gloomy Christianity is irreconcilable human relationships. These two Christian sisters did not want to get along with each other; perhaps they had a grudge match.

A husband and a wife do not want to reconcile their differences. A mother and father do not want to reconcile their differences with a child. Human relationship strife is one of the primary reasons for a Christian's gloomy blues.

"Nobody understands me," you say. "She doesn't appreciate what I have done." Let me pay my respects to this whole mentality of "You haven't sat in my seat," "You haven't been in my shoes," or "You haven't walked a mile in my moccasins." There is no possible way that I can sit in your seat and know all of your problems! No other human being has ever been "you," nor will any other human being ever be "you." No one will ever have your fingerprint or your same DNA strand. God created you as a uniquely individual person, and nobody will ever understand you completely—nobody, that is, except the Lord Jesus Christ, Who was your pattern when God created you.

Because no human being will ever have complete understanding of certain situations that life brings, God provides a pattern to follow when dealing with those problems. The entire Bible is filled with examples that were written for our admonition. God wants the generations of mankind to look at all the stories He put in the Bible so we could learn from the mistakes of others. For some reason, mankind doesn't seem to realize he does not have to experience everything to learn from it. Experience is **not** the best teacher; someone else's experience is!

Believe me, I don't have to go through a fiery furnace to know my God is able to deliver me. I don't have to cross the Red Sea to know my God is capable of parting the waters. I don't have to march around Jericho to know that God can bring down the walls of depression and sadness and grief and torment. I don't have to go through Daniel's den of lions. I don't have to experience all the troubles the people in the Bible went through. Why? I know God is a very capable God.

Oh, for a generation of God's people who would realize the God they serve is as capable as He was in the Old Testament days! Instead, they shut their Bible and say, "But you have never been through what I am going through."

True, I probably have not gone through what you have gone through, and you probably haven't gone through what I have gone through, but we have a God Who knows exactly what you are going through! However, instead of going to God, His promises, His indwelling Holy Spirit, His Book, and choosing to rejoice, you reject God, His Bible, and His promises! You choose the blues, the gloom, and the depression; and you say, "Nobody understands me." Rejoicing is not a matter of finding a human being to whom you can talk; it is a turning to a Christ Who can deliver you! We turn to sourness, bitterness, anger, gloominess, and depression because we will not turn to the answer that Christ gives in His Book.

As a result, we have human strife which is caused principally by the inability to understand what another is going through. Human strife places self in the center of the universe. When dealing with the extremes of mankind, on one side is self-pity and on the other side is self-pride. The person who is full of self-pity is constantly depressed, feels unworthy and unqualified, lives a life of constant comparison, and bemoans the lack of understanding and trust he receives. On the other side of the coin, the person full of self-pride is arrogant, cocky, rude to others, and proclaims, "I am the big man." People who are full of self-pride and self-pity have the same problem—self! Christian, when you put yourself in the center of the world, you will have a self-destructing world.

Euodias and Syntyche were not getting along because each thought the other one did not understand her situation. Why are Christians down in the mouth, gloomy, and sad? Quite simply because they do not get along with each other. Would you like to cure most of the depression teenagers suffer? Their parents should stay married and get along. Holding grudges causes feelings of frustration. When a person forgives, he lets go of hurts and bitterness. Couples who feud, fight, and fume need to lay down their weapons and make a choice to be joyful!

Every person consciously makes a choice! If you are gloomy, miserable, sour, unhappy, unkind, and bitter, you choose to be that way—on purpose! Stop using that age-old excuse, "You don't know what circumstances I am going through."

I guess that means God cannot deliver you from the fiery furnace like He delivered Shadrach, Meshach, and Abed-nego. I guess God couldn't deliver you at a Red Sea crossing. I guess God isn't able to bring down the walls of Jericho for you. Every promise in the Book is mine, and I choose to believe His promises!

2. The presence or absence of success or luck is not a condition for joy. In Philippians 4:2, God tells us through the meaning of the names of Euodias and Syntyche what not to trust for joy. The name *Euodias* means "success." *Syntyche* means "luck" or "fortune." A depressed person says, "I am not very lucky; that is why I am not very happy." But God says that being joyful has nothing to do with how lucky a person is. Being joyful also has nothing to do with how successful a person is. As a matter of fact, in this particular passage, "success" and "luck" were feuding with each other!

Euodias was not very joyful because success has never brought long-term joy to anyone. The Bible says, *"Rejoice in the Lord"*—not in your success; *"Rejoice in the Lord"*—not in your fortune; *"Rejoice in the Lord"*—not in your good looks. *"Rejoice in the Lord alway: and again I say, Rejoice,"* has nothing to do with success or luck. Rather, it has everything to do with the Lord Jesus Christ because joy comes from Jesus.

It is about time Christians stop thinking, "If I just win the lottery one time." Gamblers are some of the most unhappy people I have ever met in all my life. They come to my office (as one man did) and say, "I just gambled away my house." For some reason that man did not have the joy of the Lord on his face. Believe me, he did not walk in to my office and gleefully declare, "Pastor, I just lost my house gambling! I am a happy man!" Not on your life! He was a very sad brother in Christ who suddenly forgot that he was saved and had a very powerful God. He had gambled with trying to be successful, but luck and success will never bring joy because joy is a choice.

Even though Euodias was successful, and Syntyche was lucky, neither lady was happy because success and luck have never brought anyone long-term joy. The presence or absence of either success or luck is not a condition for joy.

3. The absence of prayer and praise brings sadness, grief, and depression. Philippians 4:6 and 7, *"Be careful for nothing; but in every thing by prayer and supplication with thanksgiving let your requests be made known unto God. And the peace of God, which passeth all understanding, shall keep your hearts and minds through Christ Jesus."* The word *careful* means "full of anxiety." The first part of Philippians 4:6 is telling the Christian not to be full of care, upset, or be nervous. We need not be nervous for anything. I cannot make it any simpler than what God's Word says: the absence of prayer and praise will bring sadness and grief.

I absolutely marvel that for the most part, those with whom I counsel are the gloomiest, most downhearted people who wear the saddest expressions. I have to wonder if they ever praise God. I have to wonder, "Is God that bad to them?"

I guess I just have a different genetic code. God must have assembled my wiring just a little differently. I believe it is the greatest privilege in the world to be alive! Every morning when I lift my heart toward Heaven and pray in my private worship area, I say, "God I want to thank You for this incredible privilege to have the adventure called living." Somehow I think the privilege of living outweighs all the bad that goes with it.

On the highway of life, sometimes we hit some speed bumps

that knock our front end out of alignment. The tendency is to take one or two of the so-called big speed bumps and let that cloud rain on everything else in life. If there is a cloud in your life, praise God that outside of that cloud the sunshine is sparkling brightly! By the way, if there is a cloud in your life, rain isn't so bad either! Gray skies or blue skies, I love them all! I'm thankful to be alive!

Some people ask, "What is so good about being alive? It would be a good thing if I had never been born."

Is that your attitude toward your Creator? Is that how you thank God for giving you life to live and breath to breathe?

When I feel the clouds gathering, I practice a ritual. For instance, I look at the marvel called my hand. I open and close it, and say, "It is so much fun just moving that!" I walk around and say, "I surely enjoy being mobile!" I peel off the wrapper of a Butterfinger candy bar, enjoy smelling the chocolate and the peanut butter, bite into it, and just savor the taste. I cannot help but think that life doesn't get any better than this! God is so good!

I pick up the Bible and think, "I can read the Bible. I have a Book full of wonderful promises, and I have eyes with which to read them!" I can hear! Thank God, I have two ears with which to hear. I have a wife who loves me. I have children who love me. I have a congregation of people who love the Lord Jesus Christ! I count my blessings! An attitude of hopelessness and helplessness has a very difficult time contending with an attitude of gratitude. After a half hour of thinking how good God is, I say, "I don't know where the gloom has gone; everything is bright and sunshiny outside!" Rejoicing is a choice!

"You don't know what **I** am going through." The key word is "**I**." Shadrach, Meshach and Abed-nego could easily have said the same thing when they were sentenced to the fiery furnace. After all, turning up the air-conditioning was not an option for them! Rather than saying, "You don't know what **we** are going through," they declared, "…*our God whom we serve is able to deliver us from* *the burning fiery furnace....*" (Daniel 3:17) In anger, King Nebuchadnezzar ordered their deaths and watched their prediction come true! *"Did not we cast three men bound into the midst of the fire?"* Nebuchadnezzar asked. *"They answered and said unto the king, True, O King."* (Daniel 3:24)

"He [Nebuchadnezzar] answered and said, Lo, I see four men loose...and the form of the fourth is like the Son of God." (Daniel 3:25)

Why was the fourth man like the Son of God? Because He **was** the Son of God! Jesus was going through the trial with Shadrach, Meshach, and Abed-nego, just like He will go through any trial with us!

For some reason, we think it is so much easier to fret and worry than to fall on our face and pray. If it is so much easier to gripe and groan, why does it take fewer facial muscles to smile than it does to frown? Smile, and reduce the pressure on your face! Act happy, fake it if you have to. Choose to rejoice! Too many Christians have not learned the simple exercise of falling on their face and going to prayer to the One Who can make a difference.

After a long day of counseling and reading letters full of problems, sometimes I feel oppressed by all of the problems I encounter. I feel depressed by all the pressure of helping others. Sometimes I walk around the office and talk to God. "Lord, I feel oppressed and depressed. Please help me, I feel so pressured! It's like You have abandoned me." I go to that place in my office where I fall on my face and I start praying. I lie on my face and talk a while to God. Then I listen as He talks to me. I pray, and I listen; I pray, and I listen; I rise from the floor and say, "I am living! Thanks, God! All those burdens are gone! The oppression and depression are gone. I am so impressed with Your greatness, God."

For some, it is a whole lot easier to fret than to go to God. It is easier to pick up the phone and gripe to someone "with skin," and to say, "You don't understand what I am going through." I know Someone Who does!

"O what peace we often forfeit,
O what needless pain we bear,
All because we do not carry
Everything to God in prayer."

"I have tried prayer," you declare.

I contend if you tried prayer as much as you have tried Prozac or Paxil you would be happy. Paxil or Prozac work approximately 60 percent of the time, and as soon as people are weaned off these drugs, they tend to relapse. Why? Because drugs do not work forever. Instead, they dull your senses, numb your feelings, and sedate you through life. The people who "survive" with the help of these drugs, say, "I am not depressed. I am not impressed. I am nothing, and I just feel pressed." People who are on antidepressants are numb.

"A person's mood is like a symphony, and serotonin is the conductor's baton. Other neurotransmitters help us know our stomachs are full; serotonin tells us whether we feel satisfied. Other chemicals help us perceive the water level in a glass; serotonin helps us decide whether it's half full or half empty.[13]

Depression has always existed. "In the Old Testament, King Saul, exhibiting classic signs of depression, is troubled by an 'evil spirit.' "[14] Saul's troubled spirit was soothed when he listened to David's music; however, when Saul devised hatred and evil in his heart against David, the depression returned to haunt him.

Depression is a direct result of what you are thinking. What are you thinking about? Do you think about prayer and praise and taking time to be holy?

Some people are depressed because of the kind of music they enjoy. Bad music is not a substitute for good music. Rather, bad music is a substitute for the Bible and the preaching of God's Word. For too many years, the message has been that people listen to bad music because not enough good music is available. Wrong! The reason people listen to bad music is because they have a sorrowful spirit. They are heavy of spirit because they are not in the Word of God nor are they listening to preaching.

If listening to rock music alleviates depression, please explain to me why rock music, depression, and suicide are so intrinsically linked. In a study from 1966 to 2000, more than 55 rockers from the ages of 18 to 58 committed suicide. Of these fifty-five, nineteen shot themselves, ten overdosed on drugs, eight chose death by hanging, three jumped from buildings, and the methods the others chose were not given. Allow me to share just one scene from the depressed world of rock music:

> Kurt Cobain, leader of Nirvana, blasted himself in the head with a shotgun in a room above his garage in April 1994, at age 27. His body was not found until three days later. Cobain's first band was called Fecal Matter. He decorated his first apartment with blood-spattered baby dolls hanging by their necks and spray-painted his neighborhood with the words "Abort Christ," and "God is gay." There was garbage and rotting food all over his Seattle house. When the Cobains tried to hire some help, the maid walked into their house, then ran out screaming, "Satan lives here!"[15]

Turning to rock music will not relieve depression! The lyrics are full of suicide, death, and drugs. No wonder the life of a rock music addict is characterized by heaviness and darkness!

I believe the way to break the habit of listening to rock music is to stop listening to all music—even good music—for six months. Instead, listen to the Bible on CD and to preaching tapes day and night. What you need is the Word of God! The Word of God is the method God has used to do His work! If God can use the Word to put the sun in the sky, then God can surely put sunshine in your heart too! He will do that by the Word of God. Trying to get off bad music by listening to good music will not work. Good music is not the correct substitute; the right substitute is preaching. Why? The Bible says God has chosen preaching to manifest His Word.

I personally believe that Attention Deficit Disorder (ADD) and Attention-Deficit/Hyperactivity Disorder (ADHD) is the direct result of people not giving attention to the Lord of glory. An excessive amount of hype about these disorders has flooded our world today. *The Diagnostic and Statistical Manual of Mental Disorders, Fourth Edition Text Revision (DSM-IV-TR)* lists the following criteria for Attention-Deficit/Hyperactivity Disorder:

Six (or more) of the following symptoms of inattention have persisted for at least 6 months to a degree that is maladaptive and inconsistent with developmental level:

Inattention:

(a) often fails to give close attention to details or makes careless mistakes in schoolwork, work, or other activities

(b) often has difficulty sustaining attention in tasks or play activities

(c) often does not seem to listen when spoken to directly

(d) often does not follow through on instructions and fails to finish schoolwork, chores, or duties in the workplace (not due to oppositional behavior or failure to understand instructions)

(e) often has difficulty organizing tasks and activities

(f) often avoids, dislikes, or is reluctant to engage in tasks that require sustained mental effort (such as schoolwork or homework)

(g) often loses things necessary for tasks or activities (e.g., toys, school assignments, pencils, books, or tools)

(h) is often easily distracted by extraneous stimuli

(i) is often forgetful in daily activities[16]

The prescription drug of choice for ADD and ADHD has been Ritalin. "This [ADD or ADHD] is something that can be corrected nutritionally. After all, children weren't born with Ritalin in their brains—they certainly don't have a Ritalin deficiency."[17] Who had even heard of ADD or ADHD 50 years ago?

According to federal studies, the rate of Ritalin use in the United States is five times higher than in the rest of the world.

Researchers at Johns Hopkins University School of Medicine calculate that the number of youngsters taking Ritalin has grown two and a half times since 1990. Among the estimated 88 million children between the ages of five and fourteen, approximately 1.3 million take Ritalin on a regular basis. As a result, sales of the drug have topped $350 million a year. This astounding growth has caused many experts to suggest that Ritalin is overprescribed, and it can't be denied that many children currently taking Ritalin probably don't need it.[18]

Common causes for symptoms of ADD and ADHD are favorite foods and/or contact with dust, mold, pollen, and chemicals. The proper use of nutrients often enables the body to withstand adverse environmental exposures and problematic foods with much less difficulty.[19] Could an adverse amount of television viewing, an overabundance of sugar-laden foods, and lack of proper discipline have any bearing on the high incidence of ADD and ADHD?

Not only has Ritalin invaded the lives of our children because of ADD and ADHD, the drug has become an obsession to recreational drug users because of its availability. In people without ADHD, Ritalin in high doses can result in a heightened sense of awareness and even euphoria. It can also cause nervousness, irritability, and agitation. Ritalin abuse is at an all-time high. Ritalin is easy to find on the street, where it's commonly known as "Vitamin R," and fairly inexpensive to buy—about $1 to $5 a pill. Some Ritalin abusers buy the drug directly from children and adults who receive it legitimately.[20]

With all the negative reporting flooding the nation about Ritalin and its side effects, a new drug called Strattera was developed. The following news bulletin was released about this so-called "wonder drug":

About two million patients—adults and children—have been prescribed Strattera since it became available. Strattera won praise from some doctors and parents when it became available in 2003 as an attention deficit disorder (ADD) and attention deficit hyperactivity disorder (ADHD) treatment because, unlike Ritalin, it is not a stimulant, a class of drugs that can be addictive. But its chemical makeup is similar to certain antidepressants, which were found to have a connection to an increased risk of suicide. ADHD affects as many as 7 percent of school-aged children and 4 percent of adults in the United States.[21]

Again, I believe that God gave us medical doctors and all the wonders of the medical world. However, we must look at these situations through the eyes of God and seek results His way. One way is by eating properly and using nutritional supplements.

Good nutrition, plus taking vitamin and mineral supplements, supports the healing of your brain and body. Deficiencies of vitamins and minerals contribute to not only depression, but less-than-optimal mental performance. Consider taking a vitamin B-complex twice daily. Deficiencies of B_1, B_2, and B_6 can cause depression. Vitamin B_{12} deficiency can cause depression, neurological problems, and anemia. Vitamin C twice daily helps combat stress and strengthens your immune system. Drink at least eight 8-ounce glasses of water a day.[22]

I also believe depression is the result of people not being impressed by the supernatural Spirit of the living God. Try listening to some preaching tapes for six months, and you will have joy! Paul said, "*I can do all things through Christ which strengtheneth me.*" (Philippians 4:13) Rejoicing is your choice. In fact, everything in the Christian life is a choice.

You even become a Christian by choice. You are not born saved because your family is Christian. You do not get saved because of a religious experience. Rather, you choose to receive the Lord Jesus Christ as your Saviour. You say, "I choose Jesus."

Two thousand years ago the Son of the Living God, Jesus Christ, came from Heaven to earth, put on a man's body, and walked among mankind for 33½ years. By the miracles and the deeds He performed, He proved He was none other than that Son of the Living God. He was crucified by mankind, and He hung on the cross as your sin and my sin was poured on His body. He dipped His soul in Hell and became a human divine sacrifice for all of mankind's sin. He was buried, and three days later He rose from the grave in mighty triumph! He is alive in Heaven and sits at the right hand of the Father. He knows you. He wants to save you. He loves you. John 3:16 says, *"For God so loved the world, that he gave his only begotten Son...."* If I could, I would choose Christ for every person. Unfortunately, I cannot. I cannot choose Christ for any person. You have to choose Him for yourself.

When I was five years old, I chose Jesus Christ as my Saviour, and that wise choice has made all the difference in the world. When I was going through some sad and depressing times, I picked up His Book and said, "God, that is the Book I choose. You are the Christ I choose."

Not only did I choose Christ, I made joy my choice. I don't have a gloomy attitude, and it is not because I am a great Christian. I consciously made the choice to rejoice.

If I could, I would choose joy for every person. However, as much as I would like to, I cannot choose joy for anyone. Sad, depressed, lonely, grief-stricken, bitter, unhappy, miserable Christian, choose to rejoice! To rejoice is your choice!

"Great joy, especially after a sudden change of circumstances, is apt to be silent, and dwells rather in the heart than on the tongue."

– Henry Fielding

2

Learning to Rejoice

Suggested Reading:
Philippians 4:1-13

In chapter one, I said it is your decision whether you want to be depressed, unhappy, and sad or whether you want to be full of joy and gladness. Rejoicing is a choice each person must make.

I believe learning to rejoice is partly a science, partly an art. I also believe that Christians must learn how to rejoice. Unfortunately, rejoicing does not come as standard equipment with salvation; it is an accessory listed on the options list. You have to want to learn it and add it to your life, and I believe you have to ask God for it. I think the availability and the potential is there for learning how to rejoice. You have to choose rejoicing.

"Joy is not in things; it is in us."
–Richard Wagner

Many reach a certain point in their life where they are doing fine "under the circumstances." "I will manage, I will get by," would be their standard reply. We could go to almost any story in the Bible and find someone who is managing—under the circumstances.

Ask Joseph how he is doing as he is imprisoned in the dungeon. He could probably say, "I suppose I am getting by—under the circumstances. I am managing."

Ask Joshua how he is doing as he waits patiently for Moses on Mount Sinai to meet with God and get the Ten Commandments while the children of Israel are holding a rock concert and making havoc of God's laws.

He might say, "I am confused. My leader is on the mountain communing with God. He has no idea what is happening with the people here. I don't quite know where I fit in, but I guess I am managing—under the circumstances."

> "The greatest Christians in history seem to say that their sufferings ended up bringing them the closest to God—so this is the best thing that could happen—not the worst."
> –Peter Kreeft

When Jesus Christ was on the cross and His disciples were hiding from the Roman soldiers and the temple guard, ask Peter, James, and John how they were doing. They might have replied, "Everyone hates us, and the Romans have taken our leader. I guess we are doing all right—under the circumstances."

In nearly every Bible story, we can find someone who could say, "I guess I am surviving, and I guess I am managing—under the circumstances."

However, that theme is **not** what God emphasized in His Word. For some reason God is not very interested in a Christian's managing or getting by or surviving or doing okay under the circumstances. Rather, God orders the Christian to get out from underneath the circumstances, get on top of things, and live the victorious Christian life! God wants His people to rejoice! God didn't say, "Rejoice in the Lord occasionally when you get around to it or when circumstances provide, and again I say, think about rejoicing." No! God says, *"Rejoice in the Lord always: and again I say, Rejoice."*

Of course, rejoicing does not always mean a person will have a big laugh on his face. It means rejoicing in the Lord always.

1. A great hindrance to joy is magnifying circumstances over grace. One of the great lessons every Christian can learn about rejoicing is not to magnify his circumstances above the grace of God. So often when a Christian looks at a circumstance, he sees it as a mountain peak in relative proportion to the grace of God.

Christians tend to minimize this tangible called grace. What exactly is grace? I believe grace is the undeserved kindness of God. I believe it is God's being good to us when we don't deserve God's being good to us.

What often happens is when we have a negative in our life, we magnify that negative to the point that we stop seeing all the good things God is doing for us when we don't deserve those good things. As soon as we start magnifying the bad over the good that God is still doing for us, we have magnified circumstances above grace. In so doing, we have just robbed ourselves of joy.

We feel the circumstances of life are so great that they tip the

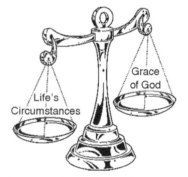

Joy is
the grace of God
counterbalancing the
circumstances of life.

scales to the point that eventually grace cannot support it. However, the Bible says that the grace of God is more than sufficient. "*My grace is sufficient...,*" God said in II Corinthians 12:9.

In the First Baptist Church of Hammond at almost the same time, we had two families who had to say goodbye to little babies who were tragically and suddenly taken to Heaven seemingly prematurely. I sat with each family in a hospital emergency room and watched both sets of parents endure the profound loss of a baby. God's grace was written all over these grieving good people. I marveled at how they did not let the circumstance outweigh the grace. The tears were abundant, and the deep sadness was evident, but God's grace overshadowed the heartbreaking circumstance. Both couples were very aware that God was still being good to them. By the way, God is still good to us even when we don't think God is being good to us. I was proud to pastor these two young couples who allowed God's wonderful grace to counterbalance their dreadful loss.

One of the great missing elements in people who are not rejoicing Christians is the awareness of the goodness of God. Charles G. Finney (1792-1875), the great revival preacher who served as president of Oberlin College from 1851 to 1866, said, "Revival is a fresh awareness of the presence of God."

What will revive a Christian's soul in the midst of a mountain-peak circumstance such as the grief of losing a loved one, the grief of the word cancer smiting a loved one's soul, or discord striking in the harmony of life is still realizing that in the midst of the sadness, the grief, and the negativity there is a great God Who is still being good to you when all the world is seemingly being bad. The whole world might walk out on you, but the grace of God never leaves you! The grace of God charms away those huge mountain peaks! When you realize that God is still good to you even when you don't deserve it, somehow it overbalances the unwanted circumstance.

However, when we see cancer as being bigger than grace or a heart attack as being bigger than grace or marital problems as being bigger than grace, we are taking our so-called little problems and placing a big magnifying glass on them. In so doing, we have made that circumstance so big that God cannot possibly fix the problem! Take away the magnifying glass, and look at those problems through the eyes of the grace of an Almighty God. Realize that His grace is ten thousand times bigger than all your problems put together! Realize that God is still being good to you in spite of life's difficulties! After all, you are breathing His air. The proper mix of oxygen was given to you by the God Whom

"If we had no winter, the spring would not be so pleasant; if we did not sometimes taste of adversity, prosperity would not be so welcome."
–Anne Bradstreet"

you don't believe cares about you. When you shake a defiant fist at God and cry out in anger, "What are You doing to me?" remember that fist was created by the God Who allows you to defiantly shake it at Him. God is so good to you—even when you don't think He is! God's grace is always abundant.

As the songwriter wrote of grace so beautifully:

"There's been grace for every trial,
There's been grace for every mile,
There's been grace sufficient from His vast supply.
Grace to make my heart more tender,
Grace to love and pray for sinners,
But there'll be new grace when it's my time to die.

Grace not yet discovered, grace not yet uncovered,
Grace from His bountiful store.
Grace to cross the river, grace to face forever,
There'll be new grace I've not needed before."

Yes, God will give new grace for every trial we face in life. Unfortunately, what happens so often is that we refuse to let God's grace be magnified in our life. We refuse to look at all the good God is doing for us. We magnify the one bitter pill that is hard to take, and we allow that bitter pill to alter all of our life!

I have watched people react to that one singular bad event that comes in life. It might be a mother and father who divorce and shatter their children's secure home life. It might be a financial setback for a husband with a supposedly secure job who is suddenly and inexplicably let go from employment where he had a secure retirement. You might lose everything that man can give you. You might lose your health. You might lose your wealth. You might lose your friends. You might lose your family, but you cannot lose the grace of God!

The grace of God—the goodness of God when you don't

deserve it—is always there for you. God is a good God. When the trials of life in the form of letters and lawsuits meet me in my office, I say, "Thank You, God, for the sight You gave me to read the words. Thank You, God, for the brain cells that You gave me to understand them. Thank You, God, for being good all the time! Unkind letters and frivolous lawsuits do not matter with You in control!"

Perhaps in your case the bills are piled high with not enough money at the end of the month to care for them. Then you also unexpectedly got laid off just before the Christmas holidays. Your wife is undergoing cancer tests, and you are all fretting. In spite of all the fears and fretting, isn't God still being good to you? The bottom line is we must magnify the goodness of God and we stop magnifying the problems in our life. There are no problems bigger than God!

2. Another hindrance to joy is when we stop learning and just stop growing. Paul said in Philippians 4:11, "*I have learned....*" Verse 12 says, "*I know how to... in all things I am instructed....*" In his later years, Paul, the great theologian who wrote half of the New Testament, said, "I am still learning how to have joy." He wrote, "*I know both how to be abased, and I know how to abound.*" He was saying that he had learned something he did not previously know.

Paul said in this Scripture that he had learned something that few Christians understand: the importance of continued growth. Like Paul, we can continue to learn. However, so often a Christian is so chained to his body of death. In his early years when his body is fresh and young, he grows and grows and grows; his soul is also growing. The curiosity of his soul is learning, reading books, and being introduced to a big, bright, beautiful world. He has yet to be introduced to cancer, bankruptcy, divorce, hatred, jealousy, envy, anger, and hostility. He only knows there is a beautiful butterfly to chase, a flower to smell, a deer to watch, a

"Find ecstasy in life; the mere sense of living is joy enough." –Emily Dickinson

friend to enjoy—all the fun things in life to explore.

When we reach the middle years, the body stops growing. Changing enters. The eyesight weakens, the joints start aching, and the hair turns gray. As the body to which we are chained stops growing, the soul also stops growing. You begin thinking you know all that you need to know.

As a result, middle-aged people become conceited, arrogant, and proud. They think they have learned all that they need to learn, and they believe everything in their life is under control— their finances, their marriage, their children, etc. The bottom line is that middle-aged Christians usually stop growing; and when God allows the bigger problems to enter their lives, because they have stopped growing, they are consequently unable to handle the trials.

This natural progression is why seniors fit into one of two categories: (1) senior saints, or (2) bitter, grumpy, and groaning old Christians with nothing constructive to say. On the other hand, some of the sweetest people in the world are senior saints whose souls kept on growing when the body started shutting down.

As we all know, the body is limited in how long it will be on this earth. However, the soul is ageless and eternal! That ageless soul is why you talk to seniors who are incredibly happy and who still feel like kids. They are! Their soul hasn't grown any older!

The only way to learn how to rejoice is by continuing to learn. When you stop learning and growing, you stop rejoicing. By continuing to grow, you are enabled to meet the problems of life without being overwhelmed. If you stop growing, you are easily overwhelmed by life's problem. You did not continue to grow up and learn to face the problems that come with life.

When you keep growing by reading your Bible daily, praying every day, reading good books and literature, listening to preaching, walking with God, and developing good Christian friendships, you can face every problem that comes into your life. Don't stop growing just because your body starts growing old. Your soul never has to grow up.

We have a senior saint in First Baptist Church named Mary Ruth Harrington, who at this writing is in her middle 80s. I call her "sinfully young" because she talks and acts like a 20 year old! She is full of mischief. The girls in her high school Sunday school class love her because she doesn't act like an old, worn-out woman; she is interested in them and their problems. She is happy, vivacious, and effervescent even though her body is getting old. Her soul stays young and continues to grow.

When the body gets old and the Christian stops growing, the soul stagnates. Your soul is no longer young, vivacious, and alive because you stop reaching, studying, learning, and growing; you started dying. When we stop learning, the "I can" of Philippians 4:13 becomes the "I can't!"

> "When we stop learning, the 'I can' of Philippians 4:13 becomes the 'I can't!' "

The only way *"I can do all things through Christ..."* is by the *"I have learned..."* of Philippians 4:11, 12. Sadly, some Christians cannot do because they have not learned. They have failed to realize that the aging of the body and the ending of relationships does not spell the death of a soul. If you are saved and the grace of Jesus Christ has brought salvation to your soul, and you have put your faith and confidence in Jesus Christ to take you to Heaven when you die, your soul is eternal. Your body might rest in a cemetery someday, but the Bible says you will have a brand new body to house that never-dying, ageless soul.

My predecessor and father-in-law, Dr. Jack Hyles, never became cantankerous, bitter, unhappy, or disgusted with life. In their 60s and early 70s, he and Mrs. Hyles were enjoying cruises and acting like 25-year-old newlyweds on a honeymoon! He had learned how to age. He had learned the lessons of how to lose his mama and some of his friends of a lifetime. He had learned how to accept what life makes you lose. He had learned that sometimes a person has to say goodbye to those dearest in life. He also learned that a Christian does not have to grow bitter over the losses of life. He was an amazing example of a person who never let bitterness take his happiness.

3.   **The third hindrance to joy is measuring God's goodness by the past, not the future.**   As I thought about this point, I could not help but think of my associate pastor, Dr. Johnny Colsten. Midway through 2002, he suffered a stroke that to this day causes numbness and tingling in one-half of his body. Does he measure God's goodness by his previous good health? Or should he look forward to that day when the Bible promise of a new body comes to him? *"Behold, I shew you a mystery; We shall not all sleep, but we shall all be changed, In a moment, in the twinkling of an eye, at the last trump; for the trumpet shall sound, and the dead shall be raised incorruptible, and we shall be changed."* (I Corinthians 15:51, 52) A brand-new body waits for Brother Johnny!

He has a choice to make. He can press on and believe that his best days are not behind him; rather, his greatest days are still ahead! Brother Colsten might have some bad days and possibly he will have to cross chilly Jordan alone, but beyond is the glory of the Lord Jesus Christ!

Sadly, we tend to measure God's goodness by the past, not the future. God's goodness used to be measured by decades. Then, mankind began to measure God's goodness by the calendar. Now God's goodness is being measured by the moment! For instance, we get so uptight if the traffic light doesn't turn green in a few seconds. "What are You doing to me, God? You'll make me late! Come on God, make it turn green!" However, God does not work on that level of stupidity. A little wristwatch has become some people's god. We expect God to work by our time line. However, God doesn't operate by man's wristwatch or his calendar or even by decades. *"But, beloved, be not ignorant of this one thing, that one day is with the Lord as a thousand years, and a thousand years as one day."* (II Peter 3:8) Sometimes we may have to wait because God's calendar is not a twelve-month calendar!

Galatians 4:4 and 5 says, *"But when the fulness of the time was* come, *God sent forth his Son, made of a woman, made under the law, To redeem them that were under the law, that we might receive the adoption of sons."* It took God 4,000 years to wait for the fulness of time. Even though God does not work on man's timetable, God does work, He still moves, and He still performs miracles. The greatest miracles are ahead, not behind us!

Some Christians lose their joy when they start looking at what they seemingly lost instead of what is coming. Every person can say, "You don't know what I had...." True, but Christian, you don't yet know what you are going to get! You have no idea what is ahead of you. Sometimes Christians get caught up in magnifying this short little life way too much. Paul said in II Corinthians 4:17, *"For our light affliction, which is but for a moment, worketh for us a far more exceeding and eternal weight of glory."* This temporary time of testing is so insignificant compared to the eternal glory that awaits the Christian beyond the grave.

The 70 years God has allotted to most Christians is just preparation for rejoicing and for learning that His blessings and promises are true! God gives a Christian 70 years to learn how to read His book and to fall in love with it. Some Christians have forgotten why they are here on earth! For the brief time I have, I am going to measure joy by the future, not by the past.

4. **The final hindrance to our not rejoicing is loving people and things more than we love the Lord Jesus Christ.** If I lose a friend for whatever reason, the Author of the Living Word promises He will never leave me nor turn His back on me, *"...for he hath said, I will never leave thee, nor forsake thee."* (Hebrews 13:5) His Book, which holds the answers to all that life brings, will never forsake me. My God is my Friend, my Coworker, my Buddy, my Companion, my Pal, and though the whole world forsake me,

"Seek your joy in what you give, and not in what you get."
–Evan Roberts

God never will walk out of my life. "Take the whole world but give me Jesus, no turning back, no turning back." When you have lost everything that anyone would ever want, there is still Someone Who will never walk out on you. Hebrews 13:8, *"Jesus Christ the same yesterday, and to day, and for ever."*

The truth of the matter is when you become more upset over losing someone or something to the point where you lose your joy, then you are revealing that you put your love in someone or something more than you did in the Bible and its Author. Our greatest affection should be reserved for the Bible. In the Daleth section, the fourth section of Psalm 119, we are told that the Bible is supposed to be an intimate lover. The Bible uses intimate language that is reserved for husbands and wives. God says that act of love is exactly what the Bible is supposed to be to the Christian—an intimate lover. We must find a sustaining power from the Word of God that supercedes what any other relationship of life could ever afford.

We must learn the art of rejoicing. We must be a people who rejoice in spite of enemies, obstacles, and the problems of life. *"Rejoice in the Lord alway: and again I say, Rejoice."* (Philippians 4:4)

*"We could never learn
to be brave and patient
if there were only joy in the world."*
–Helen Keller

3

Interrupted Joy

Suggested Reading:
I Peter 1:3-9

In the suggested reading passage, verse six is the pivotal verse. *"Wherein ye greatly rejoice, though now for a season, if need be, ye are in heaviness through manifold temptations."* The question asked is, "Where do I greatly rejoice?" In verses three through five God gives what we could call the basic diet of rejoicing. In what do you find joy? What is the oatmeal, the toast, the eggs, and the bacon, so to speak, of rejoicing? What are the staples of joy?

> "The pursuit of happiness is a most ridiculous phrase; if you pursue happiness, you'll never find it."
> – C. P. Snow

Do we find our joy in days off of work, in holidays, and in vacations? If that is the case, our joy ends when the holidays and vacations are over. However, this is not the joy to which this passage is referring.

A time comes in a person's life where his joy seems to be severely interrupted, and heaviness comes. The Bible word *heaviness* is our modern word "depression"—distress, grief, and sadness. In reality, heaviness is 180° in the opposite direction of joy. God says that heaviness is sometimes needful and necessary. In God's eyes, it is necessary to interrupt a Christian's basic diet of joy.

When our basic joy is interrupted, we must then learn to take our joy to another level. Therefore, during that interruption of joy, we must find yet another source of joy to add to our basic steady diet.

For whatever reason, your joy has been diminished, and you cannot find joy in the same basic steady diet. However, when the Christian experiences a time of heaviness, God wants him to find that other source of joy or learn the reasons for the heaviness. When that happens, God says you will spring up to a new level of joy until you are greatly rejoicing! I Peter 1:8 says, *"Whom having not seen, ye love; in whom, though now ye see him not, yet believing, ye rejoice with joy unspeakable and full of glory."* In verse 6 God says, *"Wherein ye greatly rejoice...,"* but in verse 8, *"ye rejoice with joy unspeakable"*! Greater joy came to the Christian!

Paul said he had experienced joy—great joy—then became depressed, then rebounded and found indescribable joy. In other words, Paul found a new level of joy. No language can put this cycle in a proper perspective. The whole Christian life is learning how to find your joy, letting the joy be pushed down in heaviness, then springing up into greater joy, being pushed down in heaviness, and then springing up in greater joy until the Christian can say, "My joy is at a level that I cannot use human words to explain the happiness and joy." I believe there is a way to enjoy the Christian life on such a plane that the delightfulness can not be described. God has no limits.

The Christian wants, as the song says, "Joy unspeakable and full of glory...oh, the half has never yet been told." However, that joy unspeakable comes from joy being interrupted.

The natural normal attitude of humanity is negative. All creation sings in a minor key—a mournful sound of complaining, whining, and general discontent. However, the natural, normal attitude and emotion of the spiritual Christian should be one of joy and gladness. That kind of attitude is contrary to the world.

As I contemplate having joy unspeakable, I am reminded of a story I heard several years ago. An insurance agent, who had 30 employees, noticed that his sales were on a steady, downward spiral. He had no idea what the answer was to his problem. He tried incentives and rewards; however, nothing seemed to be working. One day he went to work quite early and merely observed his employees as they came in to work. In five minutes he knew exactly what the problem was. He called an emergency meeting. He said, "We have a new policy starting today. You will walk into my office with a smile on your face, joy in your heart, courtesy and kindness in your voice, or you are fired! You will either be fired up with enthusiasm, or you will be fired with enthusiasm. I would rather have you come in five, ten, or fifteen minutes late or call in sick for a half day than to come in with a whiny attitude." The next month their sales went up 70 percent! Having a joy mentality will work.

> "Laughter is the jam on the toast of life. It adds flavor, keeps it from being too dry, and makes it easier to swallow."
> –Diane Johnson

Why do some churches grow and other churches stagnate or die? I know of some soul-winning churches with bus ministries that are dying. Years ago I asked my predecessor, Brother Hyles, "What makes a growing church?"

"That is easy," he said, "an excited church member! Just find a church member who has the joy of the Lord in his heart, who is excited about his church, and spreads that joy and excitement. That church will be a growing church. Happy people, happy with their church, happy with their family, and happy with their life are the ones who bring people to church and help them grow."

The Scripture says every Christian should have a basic diet of joy. In that diet are basic ingredients that make him happy and joyful and keep him from having a negative spirit. I Peter 1:3-6 lists the four ingredients a Christian should have for joy.

1. The first ingredient of a Christian's basic joy is being born again. I Peter 1:3 says, *"Blessed be the God and Father of our Lord Jesus Christ, which according to his abundant mercy hath begotten us again...."*

A Christian needs to find a steady basic joy in being born

again. The songwriter, James P. Sullivan, described that joy so beautifully in his song," Oh! Say, But I'm Glad."

> "There is a song in my heart today,
> Something I never had;
> Jesus has taken my sins away,
> Oh! Say, but I'm glad."

Don't ever fail to find joy in being born again! Every person can begin getting joy if he realizes the wonderful truth of being born again! Remember with joy and gladness the day when you were saved!

For me, it was a September day in 1963 when I was five years old. I was sitting on the edge of the sink, and I was "shaving." My sister made me sit down on the edge of the bathtub so she could tell me how to get saved. "I never shall forget that day when Jesus washed my sins away!" Salvation is where joy starts for the Christian.

Because the world does not have salvation, they must find their joy in something else. They have to find some form of external stimulus to give them joy. They have to go to theme parks like Great America to ride some kind of exciting ride. They try to find their joy in smoking cigarettes or taking recreational drugs or drinking liquor or using some other form of external stimuli.

Thank God, I chose Jesus Christ for my Saviour, and that choice has made all the difference in the world for me! I am saved, and that is where my joy begins. Every Christian's joy should begin at receiving His priceless gift called salvation.

2. The second ingredient of a Christian's basic joy is the knowledge that Jesus lives. I Peter 1:3 says, "*...begotten us again unto a lively hope by the resurrection of Jesus Christ from the dead.*" Alfred H. Ackley wrote,

> "I serve a risen Savior,
> He's in the world today;
> I know that He is living, whatever men may say;

I see His hand of mercy, I hear His voice of cheer,
And just the time I need Him He's always near.

He lives, He lives.
Christ Jesus lives today!
He walks with me and talks with me along life's narrow way."

The significant difference between Christianity and every other religion is that we serve a risen Saviour! Our faith is not found in a man or in an angel or in a prophet. The Christian's faith is found in Jesus. He is alive today!

3. The third ingredient of a Christian's basic joy is the knowledge that an eternal inheritance in Heaven waits for him. *"To an inheritance incorruptible, and undefiled, and that fadeth not away, reserved in heaven for you."* (I Peter 1:4) Every Christian has an eternal inheritance in Heaven waiting for him.

Remember the man who gambled away his house in chapter one? To that man I said, "You have lost everything you can possibly lose on earth, but you can **never** lose the eternal inheritance waiting for you in Heaven!

An undefiled, never tainted, never spoiled inheritance is reserved in Heaven for every child of God. I like what Dr. Russell Anderson, the co-founder of Hyles-Anderson College and a multimillionaire, says about his earthly wealth. "At the reading of my will, I want all my loved ones, friends, and family to be present. My will is going to say, 'I, Russell Anderson, being of sound mind, gave it all away.' I am trying to give away all the money I have."

"Joy has nothing to do with material things or with a man's outward circumstances...a man living in the lap of luxury can be wretched, and a man in the depths of poverty can overflow with joy."
–William Barclay

I heard a man on a radio talk show say, "When the shares for a certain company were $105 a share, I bought 4,000 shares."

The talk show host said, "Wow! That is $400,000!"

The man being interviewed then said, "My stock is worth $1.08 per share right now. I have lost just about $400,000."

The host asked, "How are you doing?"

The formerly wealthy man answered, "How do you think I am doing?" That man never learned that stock values never decline in Heaven!

I often think about the story Brother Hyles told of flying on the same airplane with Russell Anderson. He noticed that Dr. Anderson was carefully reading the business section of the *Wall Street Journal*. Finally he asked, "Russ, what are you doing?"

Brother Anderson said, "I am checking my investments." He looked at Brother Hyles and noticed he was reading his King James Bible. "What are you doing, Dr. Hyles?"

"I am reading about my heavenly investments," Brother Hyles answered. It's true that having heavenly investments is more important than having earthly investments, but Christians need to make earthly investments to build those heavenly investments!

No matter how much wealth and material possessions a person accumulates on this earth, nothing can be compared with the glory that shall be hereafter. We have an inheritance!

4. The fourth ingredient of a Christian's basic joy is the knowledge that, as a believer, he has eternal security. *"Who are kept by the power of God through faith unto salvation ready to be revealed in the last time."* (I Peter 1:5) As a Christian, I have eternal security! I am kept by the power of God.

Once you are saved, you never lose that gift of salvation. *"All that the Father giveth me shall come to me; and him that cometh to me I will in no wise cast out."* (John 6:37) He gives you eternal life, not temporary life for this earthly life only, but eternal, everlasting life.

We can never lose what God has for us. The second verse of the wonderful Philip P. Bliss song, "Jesus Loves Even Me" says,

"Tho I forget Him and wander away,
Still He doth love me wherever I stray;
Back to His dear loving arms would I flee,
When I remember that Jesus loves me!"

No matter how far a Christian strays from God, he can never stray from the power of God! He can try to run in sin, but the blood of Jesus Christ, God's Son, cleanses him from all sin!

God has promised not to impute (credit to my account) unrighteousness that I commit. God said in Romans 4:8, *"Blessed is the man to whom the Lord will not impute sin."* No act of unrighteousness is marked on my account because my record was cared for at Calvary! At Calvary He washed away all my sins from my record and put the righteousness of Jesus Christ on my record! Even though a Christian sins against Him, shames Him, and embarrasses Him, He still says, "I see the righteousness of God."

What is the basic general diet for joy? You have to know you are born again. You have to understand that Jesus lives. You have to understand that you have an inheritance that is undefiled and cannot be taken from you. You have eternal security; you can never lose that salvation. In all this we Christians can rejoice, and through these things we can learn to greatly rejoice.

No Christian says, "To be honest with you, I wish I weren't saved. I wish I would go to Hell." The only people who would make such a ludicrous statement are unsaved people who do not know how good it is to be saved. The worst day for the Christian is a whole lot better than a good day for the unsaved man.

What happens when this basic diet of joy is interrupted at the hand of God? God will interrupt the Christian's joy and bring a **season** of heaviness—not a life of heaviness. *"Wherein ye greatly rejoice, though now for a season, if need be, ye are in heaviness through manifold temptations."* (I Peter 1:6) In this verse God says it is necessary sometimes to have a season of heaviness.

Paul said that he was in constant heaviness for his unsaved loved ones—the Israelites. On the other hand, he was also the same man who said, *"Rejoice in the Lord alway: and again I say, Rejoice."* Just like the Apostle Paul embraced heaviness, every Christian must endure seasons of heaviness.

"Joy is the internal confidence and gladness I feel that comes from understanding the Word of God."

This concept is so important to understand, but in order to understand fully, we must first understand what joy really is. Joy is the internal confidence and gladness I feel that comes from understanding the Word of God. When a person understands what the Bible is teaching him, he is given a platform on which he can stand internally.

Most of what we call joy is actually external, artificial stimuli. It is the excitement we feel when riding a roller-coaster, getting off, and saying, "I just have to ride that ride again! Oh, no! Look at that long line!" How quickly the joy changes from elation to despair. It is the anticipation for Christmas and the hollow feeling at the end of Christmas Day when all that remains is used wrapping paper and boxes. The kids have left to go back to their homes, and we are left alone with our memories. These are examples of the external that often gives us a platform on which to base our joy, and that is why we are always looking for the next external bit of excitement that again brings only momentary joy. God wants us to build an internal platform on which we can stand that is rock solid—no matter what external circumstances we must face.

To be sure, the external stimuli is always a distraction, but God uses external testing to lead us to more stable spiritual truth. Because God is constantly working to build us spiritually from within, He uses multiple testings to accomplish this purpose.

You know you are saved, but your son is in the hospital. You know Jesus is alive, but why isn't He healing your son who is undergoing chemotherapy? You know you have an inheritance, but you desperately miss loved ones who are already in Heaven. You know you can't lose your salvation, but you feel the heaviness and the pressure of life all around you. Perhaps your marriage is faltering, or your children are straying, or your finances are unstable, and as a result, you feel incredibly depressed. As you face these multiple testings of life, God says, "You must change where you are finding your joy when you are in a season of heaviness."

The trials (testings) of faith are reminders from God Almighty.

We have been given an opportunity with our heaviness to prove to God how much we love Him. At that moment when we are feeling the intense pressure, how we respond right then determines whether or not we can find our "rejoicing."

The question is: What do I do when I am pushed down? Very simply, when I feel pressed down, I find my joy in the words of one of the simplest songs I know: "Jesus loves me, this I know; for the Bible tells me so!" The bottom-line basic fundamental element of all joy when the pressures of life come is knowing that Jesus loves me! When we cannot find happiness in salvation or the fact that our Saviour lives, or that we have an inheritance or that we are eternally secure, we can say with Job of old when he was in heaviness, *"For I know that my redeemer liveth...."* (Job 19:25) We can still find our joy in the fact that Jesus loves us!

When we are going through a time of heavy testing, what an opportunity we have been given to declare to the Saviour, "I told You I love You!"

> "I am not a theologian or a scholar, but I am very aware of the fact that pain is necessary to all of us. In my own life, I think I can honestly say that out of the deepest pain has come the strongest conviction of the presence of God and the love of God."
> – Elisabeth Elliot

As I mentioned in the previous chapter, Brother Johnny Colsten suffered a stroke and lives with a paralyzing numbness that affects half of his body. What an opportunity for Brother Johnny to say, "God, all these years I have served You. I told You many times that I loved You. Now you have brought the trial of sickness to my faith. That testing tells me that I told You I love you!"

Every trial we experience gives us a marvelous opportunity to remind God that our love was sincere. What a marvelous opportunity to prove that the love we had in our heart for Him is really genuine! When we look at our trials—the seasons of heaviness—we can say, "God, what a wonderful reminder You brought to me to show You my faith is real." Sometimes we tend to forget what a great privilege it is to suffer on behalf of the Christianity we believe.

> "But 'I know whom I have believed
>   and am persuaded that He is able
> To keep that which I've committed
> Unto Him against that day.' "

When we realize the heaviness comes so that we can prove that our love to God is genuine, then we will find that joy unspeakable and full of glory.

"Since you get more joy out of giving joy to others, you should put a good deal of thought into the happiness that you are able to give."
—Eleanor Roosevelt

4

Exceeding Joy

Suggested Reading:
I Peter 4:12-19

W hen our children were young, our daughter was invited to go to a party. As we were getting ready to take her, Jaclynn said, "I'm not sure I want to go. I am not sure if I am going to have a good time. What if I don't have a good time?"

My wife answered her question with a question: "Why don't you bring a good time with you?"

"Happiness depends upon ourselves."
—Aristotle

All throughout life you must make decisions. The Christian life is a matter of decisions. I personally believe the greatest power in all the world is the power of choice. A person chooses whether he wants to go to Heaven or Hell. God does not make that choice for anyone. Every person has a decision to make. He can choose to go to Heaven by choosing Jesus Christ; that choice is his alone to decide. II Peter 3:9 says, *"The Lord is not slack concerning his promise, as some men count slackness; but is longsuffering to us-ward, not willing that any should perish, but that all should come to repentance."* God's choice is to offer salvation to every person, but each individual has to choose to have salvation.

Just like we choose whether or not to be saved, we also choose everything else in the Christian life. We may not personally choose our circumstances, but we choose all the internal. We also choose how to accept circumstances. We choose how to deal with what life brings us. Having joy is also a choice.

We have to decide whether or not we will bring joy with us wherever we go. If we want to have a good time, we are supposed to bring a good time with us. For example, if a person wants to go to church and enjoy church, it is up to him. The person who gets married says, "This is my choice, and I am going to be happy with my choice." The result of thinking is happiness. However, if the person says, "I am marrying you; you better make me happy," then happiness will only occur on rare occasions. Ordering a spouse to bring happiness will not bring happiness.

We enter into the Christian life by choice, and we enjoy the Christian life by choice. As we have already determined in chapter one, we decide to rejoice by choice. The whole issue of possessing joy comes down to choosing to have joy.

Once I have made the choice to choose joy, then God begins taking that journey to find joy with me. In the previous chapter, I discovered that there are four basic ingredients of joy:

1. I am born again.
2. I serve a risen Saviour. Jesus is alive today!
3. I have an eternal inheritance waiting for me in Heaven.
4. I am eternally secure; I cannot lose my salvation.

Inevitably, that joy the Christian has chosen is tested. Just like a wristwatch tells the time, testing will come. In I Peter 4:12, the Bible says, *"Beloved, think it not strange concerning the fiery trial which is to try you, as though some strange thing happened unto you."* This verse is asking why Christians seem to think it is so peculiar when their faith or their joy is tested. The sun rises in the east and sets in the west. I do not know how to make it any plainer. If you are a born-again Christian your faith will be tested. God will tailor-make that test for you.

For instance, I know this ministry will be tested. I was discussing some of the difficulties in the ministry, and the gentleman with whom I was talking asked, "How do you handle the fact that you have over 27 lawsuits against you?"

I felt that I could give a good credible answer. One way I reconcile the multiple lawsuits is the fact that First Baptist Church is a multimillion-dollar corporation. Three separate corporations are under the leadership of our board of directors. I once had the privilege to chat with the CEO of one of the Fortune 500 companies, and I asked him, "How many lawsuits does a company like yours have?" When he said that at the last count they had roughly 4,000 lawsuits in litigation, I couldn't help but think that I was doing something right! I believe all of the lawsuits will work out in God's timing and by His will. I am not surprised when bad things happen to good people.

I am not surprised when testing comes into the lives of people. I happened to pick up an older issue of *US News and World Report* and read an alarming statistic about cancer. The article reported that one out of every two Americans will have some form of cancer in their lifetime. That statistic was so startling, I did some checking. According to the SEER (Surveillance, Epidemiology and End Results Program of the National Cancer Institute) Cancer Statistic Review, 1975-2002, males have a 45.67% chance of developing cancer in their lifetime. Females have a 38.09% chance of developing cancer in their lifetime.[1] A cancer diagnosis of some form will indeed touch the lives of many people. So will the other surprise tests of life! Why be surprised when the car breaks down? Bad things will undoubtably happen in life.

When the tests of life (or the tests of my joy) come, I am not surprised by them. When Peter wrote that Christians should not think it is strange that their joy would be tested, he had already seen the Saviour crucified. What comes into our lives cannot possibly be compared to the testing of Jesus—His suffering on a cross.

The cross is always the Christian's pivotal example, his turning point, his focus that helps him to realize how good he has it.

Everybody has problems. Peter said in I Peter 1:6, *"Wherein ye greatly rejoice, though now for a season, if need be, ye are in heaviness through manifold temptations."* The word *manifold* means "a variety" or "a whole group." Testings come in all different shapes and sizes.

Why Is the Christian's Joy Tested?

The answer is very simple. The trials of the Christian's faith and the test of his joy are there to prove the source of his joy. Testing comes principally to remind him and to validate the source of his joy. The Psalmist says in Psalm 43:4a, *"Then will I go unto the altar of God, unto God my exceeding joy."* When this Psalm was penned, David was being tested sorely. David was hiding from Saul in the cave of Adullam. He and his men were being chased by Saul like he was some wretched refuse of society. While taking refuge in that cave, he cried out to God, "Why am I being tested?" David recognized that God wanted him to realize his source of joy was God Almighty—not safety from a jealous king.

Testing comes to the first institution that God created—marriage. Why does a couple get married? For all the things that a spouse will do? For a new or remodeled house? For the spouse's provisions? No! A couple gets married for the person. A couple gets married to be with another person so when the best or the worst comes into their life, they can say to each other, "I am so glad I have you!"

On the same day I happened to counsel a married couple and an engaged couple. Basically I gave the same counsel to both couples. To the married couple I said, "Let me remind you why you got married." To the engaged couple I said, "Let me tell you why you are getting married and what the wedding day is all about." As I looked at the engaged couple, I said, "The wedding day is for the two of you. It is not for your mother. It is not all about a dress or flowers or decorations or a cake. It is about a man wanting a woman and a woman wanting a man and their wanting to be with each other. Let that be the big event of the wedding day."

The best thing about my marriage is not what my wife has provided for me. The best thing about my marriage is my wife. She provides me the satisfaction, and that is the object of my joy. I am happy because of the person with whom I get to enjoy the journey of life.

Occasionally my wife travels to ladies' meetings, and to be honest, I am very lonely without her. I said, "Lord, I just want her to be here." I thank Him just for the presence of my wife.

The big event of a person's life is not what God does for them. God surely pours many blessings on His children. God is so good to us.

I love how the congregation at Hyles Baptist Church in Chesterfield, Virginia, respond to their pastor, Brother Ron Talley. When he says, "God is good," they always say, "All the time!" Let's never forget that God is always good—all the time!

"When the hard times or the tests come, neither my position nor my possession are the source of my joy."

When the hard times or the tests come, neither my position nor my possessions are the source of my joy. Rather, my Person, Jesus Christ, is the source of my joy! I always want my tests to remind me that the reason I am a happy Christian is because I serve a risen Saviour! Jesus coming into my heart doesn't give me joy; rather, I can find my joy in Jesus Christ! Some people walk through the fiery furnace with Him but fail to realize He is there and fail to understand that He is the source of their joy.

If you lost everything that you count dear to your life right now, would you have any joy left? May I remind you, nothing can take God from you! God is testing your joy to remind you that the ultimate source of joy is Jesus Christ. God is always good! Never forget that our joy is not found in a position or possessions; it is found in the person of Jesus Christ.

If my joy is in God himself, I can continuously find joy in Him no matter what testings come my way. I can meet those obstacles knowing that they cannot hurt my source of joy which is Jesus! The test of my joy is to determine or prove the source of my joy and to establish a partnership with Christ. The Bible says in I Peter 4:13 that we can be partakers of the sufferings of Christ. Three Hebrew young men, Hananiah (Shadrach), Mishael (Meshach), and Azariah (Abed-nego) were tested severely by being placed in a fiery furnace at the command of King Nebuchadnezzar. The king looked into the fiery furnace and said to his henchman, *"Did not we cast three men bound into the midst of the fire?"* Nebuchadnezzar's men responded, *"True, O king."*

"Let my name stand among those who are willing to bear ridicule and reproach for truth's sake, and so earn some right to rejoice when the victory is won."
–Louisa May Alcott "

"Lo, I see four men loose…and the form of the fourth is like the Son of God," cried the king. (Daniel 3:23-25) The three Hebrew children learned that the test of their joy brought the partnership of Christ!

Ask yourself: "How badly do I really want to be close to God?" Do you want to know Him? Do you want to look upon His face? The way to see Jesus Christ is through the testing of your joy.

I had the privilege to visit one of our long-time deacons at First Baptist Church, who had undergone cancer surgery on his neck. This good man had a halo screwed into his skull and had to walk with a walker while he was recovering from his surgery. I was blessed to hear this rejoicing Christian man say, "The Lord is so good to me, Brother Schaap." I left that home a better man for having visited him. That deacon understands the principle that the testing of his joy is to walk in partnership with his Saviour.

I personally would not want to go through what he has faced, but I surely do want the joy he has. I have found that some of the happiest people I know are the ones who are the most severely tested and tried, those who have gone under the surgeon's knife, those who have visited the cancer clinics as patients, and those who did not know if they had a tomorrow. When you go through the deep waters of life—the deep troubles of life—the reason you go through them is to remind yourself Who is at your side. We can make it if He is at our side!

> "I don't know about tomorrow,
> I just live from day to day.
> I don't borrow from its sunshine,
> For its skies may turn to gray.
> I don't worry o'er the future,
> For I know what Jesus said,
> And today I'll walk beside Him,
> For He knows what is ahead.
>
> Many things about tomorrow,
> I don't seem to understand;
> But I know Who holds tomorrow,
> And I know Who holds my hand."

I sang that song many times since October 2000 after I had a meeting with Brother Hyles at the Lansing Bakers Square. At that crucial time, he wanted me to make a definite decision about taking his place as pastor of First Baptist Church of Hammond. Finally I said, "I won't let fear make my choice."

Thankfully he said, "I can live with that." Then he added, "In 15 months I won't be pastoring this church. I know you want me to live until I am 85. Trust me, I won't be pastoring in 15 months, maybe less." His words were prophetic; five months later we buried him.

After that meeting, I dropped him off at the church, and I drove to the college with tears running down my face. I just kept singing, "I don't know about tomorrow, I just live from day to day. I don't borrow from its sunshine, for its skies may turn to gray..." over and over and over. When I pulled into my parking space at the college, I said, "That is the answer! I know Who holds my hand!"

If we want the joy of the Lord, we will be tested because tested joy leads to exceeding joy. Tested joy brings greater joy. Tested joy brings joy unspeakable and full of glory. We need not be afraid to endure testing because the source of our joy is the person of Christ, and tested joy brings a Saviour alongside. If the way to have the Saviour walking by me and having His hand in mine is to go through the testing of joy, then bring on the test! *"That the trial of your faith, being much more precious than of gold that perisheth, though it be tried with fire, might be found unto praise and honour and glory at the appearing of Jesus Christ."* (I Peter 1:7)

> "When you are joyous, look deep into your heart, and you shall find it is only that which has given you sorrow that is giving you joy."
> –Kahil Gibran

As a young adult, Brother Hyles stood by the coffin of his father wondering why his dad had to die and go to what he believed was a Christless eternity. As he stood alone, feeling he could not go on in the future, suddenly a hand gripped his elbow. As he felt that firm grip on his arm, he turned to see who it was. Nobody was there, but Brother Hyles realized the Lord was saying, "I came to be with you."

In Acts 27 Paul sailed on a ship that he knew would encounter a tumultuous storm. In fact, he told the centurion and his crew not to sail. However, the soldiers disregarded Paul's warning and sailed anyway. In the face of the horrendous storm, the captain and his sailors began making plans to abandon the ship. Paul went into the hold below deck, began praying, and after a considerable absence, came topside and told the centurion in charge, *"Wherefore, sirs, be of good cheer: for I believe God, that it shall be even as it was told me."* (Acts 27:25)

The testing of your joy always brings the reality of your source of joy. It also brings the presence of the source of joy. The test of your joy is to remind you Who you want to bring you comfort. When the test of joy exposes you, to what do you turn in your time of greatest need? Some who are tested severely turn to the world and all that is artificial to provide that replaced joy. Others turn to the Saviour Who is waiting to walk at their side. Having exceeding joy is a choice—just like rejoicing is a choice.

People who are tested either get better or they get bitter. Those who get better realize that God + me = a majority!

Some throw a pity party, question God, and thereby expose where they found their source of joy which is definitely not in God. Those who ignore the presence of His companionship effectively block the presence of exceeding joy in their lives. Problems and testings teach us the real source of joy.

"The world is so full of care and sorrow that it is a gracious debt we owe to one another to discover the bright crystals of delight hidden in somber circumstances irksome tasks."

–Helen Keller

5

The Fruit of Sorrow

Suggested Reading:
John 16:20-24

In John 16, Jesus was just a few hours away from going to the Garden of Gethsemane and a few hours from going to Calvary. He was trying to prepare His disciples for what He knew would be the inevitable depression and sorrow that would come into their lives from His death on the cross. He shared how the world would rejoice for a time over His demise. He also shared that the reason for the world's happiness would actually be their sadness. Jesus tried to make the reasons for His death on the

"Out of suffering have emerged the strongest souls."
–Edwin H. Chapin

cross as clear to them as possible. He further explained how the world would go from being unhappy to causing much strife and tribulation for them. He assured these men whom He loved that by that time they would have learned the principle of how to take their sorrow and turn it into joy. He told them that when they understood and comprehended the whole reason for His coming, only then would their sorrow be turned to joy.

To teach this principle, Jesus gave an illustration about the discomfort and anguish a woman experiences who is giving birth to a baby. As the months slowly pass, she gains more weight and naturally grows larger with the coming baby. She becomes miserable with the waiting, and because she is miserable, those about her are miserable. She cannot wait to give birth, and when the pains start coming, the counting of contractions begins. A fast trip to the hospital soon follows. At the hospital in the maternity ward, weeping and wailing sometimes emanate from some of the birthing rooms. But then, the sorrow of the birthing process turns to joy at the birth of an infant. An incredible euphoria settles over the room as the relief and the relaxation from the stress and the pressure of the birthing process is over. The husband, the wife, and the new baby bond together. What joy they experience when the new baby arrives home! That birthing process is sorrow turned to joy. Jesus said in this illustration how sorrow is turned into joy.

I believe it is a shame how much joy is lost or wasted on unbirthed or unharvested sorrow. I believe that sorrow is another name for the seed of joy.

Someone once asked me, "What is joy?"

I believe the best definition of joy is "sorrow that has come to full term." Joy is sorrow that has been planted and is now ready for harvest. Sorrow is a seed that produces either bitterness or gladness.

In the fall as I was driving down a road adjacent to our subdivision, I saw a corn harvester picking the corn. That farmer was harvesting the fruit of his labor. In the spring that farmer had carefully sowed seeds in the ground, and then began the months of waiting for the crop to come up. Every farmer's motto is "Knee High by the Fourth of July." Like all other farmers, he hoped that the right weather conditions would prevail and cause his corn to grow knee high by the fourth of July. Perhaps he prayed for sun and the proper amount of rain. He sprayed pesticides to keep away the insects and herbicides to kill the weeds that threatened to choke the immature plants. Harvesting time had finally arrived, and that farmer was plucking the full ears of corn from his seven-foot-tall stalks. Though harvesting time requires long hours of intensive labor, no doubt he was picking that corn in gladness and joy. After all, he was reaping the full-term production of sorrow and hard work.

God brings a lot of sorrow in a person's life. Unfortunately, some people waste a lot of joy because they never properly harvest their sorrow. Many have given "birth" in sorrow and have never brought the "child" to full term. Some have even tried to force a premature birth, and sad to say, premature children don't always survive. These people live in a perpetual state of disappointment, unhappiness, grief, affliction, annoyance, grudge, pain, and depression—sorrow, if you please. These people who constantly hold a grudge, who are annoying,

> "It's surprising how many persons go through life without ever recognizing that their feelings toward other people are largely determined by their feelings toward themselves...if you're not comfortable with yourself, you cannot be comfortable with others."
> – Sydney Harris

who are afflicted, who are in constant pain emotionally, and who are incessantly depressed are people who have never learned how to bring sorrow to full term.

The happiest people with a countenance full of joy are happy every season of the year. They are as happy on April 21 or September 13 as they are on December 25. The reason they are joyful and happy is because they have learned the principle of letting sorrow produce joy. However, it is impossible to manufacture joy unless the product of sorrow is used.

Sorrow is the only proper seed of joy. Joy manufactured in any other way is artificial joy. Joy must come through travail. In the 155 references to joy in the Bible which I looked up and studied, travail is linked to joy. In II Corinthians 11:24-27 the Bible records the sorrow of the Apostle Paul which brought forth joy in his life. *"Of the Jews five times received I forty stripes save one. Thrice was I beaten with rods, once was I stoned, thrice I suffered shipwreck, a night and a day I have been in the deep; In journeyings often, in perils of waters, in perils of robbers, in perils by mine own countrymen, in perils by the heathen, in perils in the city, in perils in the wilderness, in perils in the sea, in perils among false brethren; In weariness and painfulness, in watchings often, in hunger and thirst, in fastings often, in cold and nakedness."* No wonder God used Paul to pen the book of Philippians with its incomparable fourth verse of the fourth chapter—*"Rejoice in the Lord alway; and again I say, Rejoice."* Many were saved because of Paul's sorrow. *"For what is our hope, or joy, or crown of rejoicing? Are not even ye in the presence of our Lord Jesus Christ at his coming? For ye are our glory and joy."* (I Thessalonians 2:19, 20)

> "Real joy comes not from ease or riches or from the praise of men, but from doing something worthwhile."
> –Sir Wilfred Grenfell

Time and again Paul listed sorrow as the only seed to produce godly joy. If indeed sorrow is the baby in the womb, then that baby is either aborted with remorse or delivered with joy. Aborting your sorrow brings a life of remorse, anger, and frustration. How do I know? God likens sorrow to the anguish of birthing a baby. I have counseled with many a young woman who had made a choice to abort her unborn babies. Not only can I see the anguish on her face, I can also feel the anguish of her soul. She wrings her hands and writhes in emotional pain as she remembers the abortion of her baby. No joy floods her soul.

Go to an abortion clinic and see how many people are laughing. I have talked to doctors who have turned away from the lucrative revenue that working at an abortion clinic offers because they could not live with the thought of "delivering a fetus that they murdered in the womb."

There is no joy in delivering that dead baby. For sorrow to turn to joy, the baby must be delivered with joy. Every sorrow that comes into your life through the hand of God or from the Devil either turns into anguish because you did not bring that sorrow to joy or it makes you a joyful person because you let sorrow birth into joy.

Why Sorrow Ceases to Become Joy

1. Sorrow is often aborted by self-pity. A person becomes infected with self-pity when he nurses old, unhealed wounds. He is still festering over some hurt someone inflicted on him. Perhaps some principal didn't treat him right or some teacher mishandled him in the classroom. Someone spoke unkindly or started a rumor. The person full of self-pity keeps picking at the wound and never lets it heal. He has never learned to let go of the sorrow and hurt and let it produce joy. The time has come for that sorrow to heal and bring forth fruit!

I know a young man who has a certain problem, and because of that situation he is teased and tormented by others. He came to talk with me and said, "I feel that everyone is against me. I just want to leave our Christian school and go to the public school."

"You will have to face more torment there," I offered. "Do you really think the public school kids would be kinder to you?"

"I don't know," he agonized. "I just can't stand the torment of being teased all the time."

"My brother, if you ever get over this, you will be one of the happiest Christians in the world," I explained. "You must deal with this sorrow."

As I counseled with this fine young man, I shared a story about a young man with no arms and no legs who applied to come to our college. I met him at Youth Conference. I didn't know how to greet him properly because he had no hand to shake. He was sitting in a chair—just a head and a stump of a body.

> "Suffering is the seed from which compassion grows."
> –Dolores E. McGuire

When he told me he wanted to come to Hyles-Anderson College, I was incredulous. "You want to come to our college? How are you going to walk up and down the steps?"

"I won't be walking up and down the steps," he said, "but I can walk up steps on my head. I can do anything. I can make my own bed. My mouth is phenomenally talented! Think about it, Brother

Schaap, there are a lot of great things about not having arms or legs. I never have to tie a pair of shoes, let alone buy a pair of shoes! I never have to worry about my sleeves being buttoned on my shirt."

"I thank God for my handicaps, for through them, I have found myself, my work, and my God."
–Helen Keller

To say that I was surprised by this young man's incredible attitude is an understatement. In all honesty, I thought maybe he was a fake who was just putting on. So I called his pastor and said, "I want to ask you about so and so...."

"Brother Schaap," his pastor cut in, "before you ask me a question, let me testify that he is the happiest human being I have ever met in my entire life. I have been his pastor for over ten years. Not one time in ten years have I ever seen a frown on the kid's face."

After I shared this incredible story with the young man in my office, I asked, "How is your affliction doing?"

"Pretty pale," he admitted, "compared to him, Brother Schaap."

"Self-pity measures life experiences against my personal desires rather than the spiritual truths."

In all truthfulness, I believe most of our afflictions pale in comparison to this young man who was born with no arms or legs. Yet what happens is we let our affliction turn into self-pity, and we think, "I don't deserve this." Self-pity measures life experiences against my personal desires rather than the spiritual truths. In other words, I take the experiences the world passes on to me or the Devil throws at me and what God has thrown at me, and I say, "God, that is not what I wanted." But God rejoins, "Here is what I am trying to teach you." When I measure what happens to me by what I want relative to what God wants for me, I always wind up in self-pity.

If God is working on me and trying to do something within me and I refuse to allow Him to accomplish that purpose, then I am refusing to give birth to sorrow and experience the prolonged joy that results. In effect, I am pushing away that joy.

May I ask, what do you deserve anyway? Perhaps all you want to do is to pursue and enjoy a life of happiness. Pursue it, but that kind of happiness when you have it will never bring happiness. The word *happiness* comes from the word *happenings*. In other words, things must be constantly happening to you to provide happiness.

> Sometimes the message from popular advertising seems to be that *no* unhappiness is normal—that unhappiness, as well as true depression, is, like diabetes, a biological dysfunction correctable with drugs. "We're being led to believe that you're never supposed to feel down or unhappy," says Steven Treistman, a psychopharmacologist at the University of Massachusetts Medical Center who specializes in the neural mechanisms of mood-altering drugs. "I see it in the media. It's amazing when you start to pay attention to it…happy dance, happy dance everyplace. Which would certainly make you think that if you weren't feeling that way, something's wrong with you."[1]

I contend that joy needs no external happenings; joy comes from within. The person who has joy in his heart is not affected by what is happening to him. Too many individuals are always waiting for something to happen that will bring happiness; in that case, everything about which they feel happy depends on someone else bringing happiness to them! Personally, I don't want to depend on anyone bringing happiness to me! I want to bring joy with me wherever I go.

At Christmastime we sing, "Joy to the world, the Lord is come." Sadly, this miserable world is not bringing one ounce of joy at Christmastime because most do not have the Joy-giver in their heart. An individual cannot have joy until he has joy in his heart. Joy cannot be found at the shopping mall with a lot of unhappy customers and unhappy clerks who cannot wait to clock out, hating every minute they have to work. Christmas cheer is often-times a misnomer.

I was talking to a pastor friend who asked me if I had heard from a certain person. When I said I had not and then asked about him, the pastor said, "Don't you know? He is still angry at you. Twenty years ago you rebuked his friend in your college preaching class, and he still can't get over that."

Needless to say, I was incredulous! That man is needlessly hanging on to 20-year-old wounds! What a sad way not only to lose his joy, but to rob himself of joy for 20 years! That wound of sorrow should have been birthed years ago. Deliver that child of self-pity and experience some joy! Every so-called bad thing that comes in life is an opportunity to be rejoicing. An expectant mother may feel ugly and be miserable in the last months of her pregnancy, but birthing brings an amazing happiness!

Holding grudges robs people of happiness and joy. Life is so much bigger than a petty grudge. Give birth to that sorrow and bring joy. Make peace with people. Make peace with your boss. Make peace with your children. Make peace with your family. Make peace with your grandparents. Make peace with your school. Make peace with your authorities. You are aborting joy because you can't deal with your sorrows.

2. Sorrow is aborted when we are tempted and fail again and again and again. You have failed God so many times that you feel like God doesn't love you anymore. The person who thinks that way has no idea how much God loves him! No one can ever fail Him beyond His love. Not one person can sin beyond the grace and mercies of God. The mercies of the Lord endure forever! Please don't magnify your sin above a gracious God.

You are going to fail Him because everyone fails Him. Remember Brother Hyles' masterpiece sermon, "You Can Fail, But Not Be a Failure"? He would say, "You failed, and you failed, and you failed, and you failed, and you failed, and you failed, and you failed, and you failed, and you failed, and you failed, and you failed, and you failed, and you failed, and you failed, and you failed, and you are a failure." Then he would add, "You failed, and you failed, and you failed, and you failed, and you failed, and you failed, and you failed, and you failed, and you failed, and you failed, and you failed,

and you failed, and you are a success!" He

"Ninety-nine percent of the failures come from people who have the habit of making excuses." –George Washington Carver

explained, "The difference is one person fails, runs away from the failure, and says, 'I am nothing but a failure.' Another person fails and says, 'I am learning so much. I am learning and learning and learning and learning and learning. Now, I have succeeded.' "

Why not take that failure which is nothing more than sorrow, and say, "Blessed be the Lord God Whose mercies endure forever," and start all over again! Our God is greater than any personal failure! William Lloyd George said, "He's no failure. He's not dead yet." Don't give up!

However, some people magnify their sin so big that they live in perpetual sorrow. They have magnified their sins and failures so big they have aborted sorrow. Yes, perhaps, you let your mom and daddy down. Yes, perhaps you let your spouse down. Yes, probably you let yourself down, but His mercies endure forever! *All we like sheep have gone astray; we have turned every one to his own way; and the LORD hath laid on him the iniquity of us all.* (Isaiah 53:6) Welcome to the human race! God is very aware of the fact that we are sinners! He knows we are but dust! He knows our failures!

3. Sorrow is aborted when we fail to understand the purpose of testing and trials. God is so gracious to have reasons for testings. *Trials are signs that we are a threat to the kingdom of darkness.* A pastor wrote and asked, "How do I handle people who hurt me and who I thought loved me?"

I wrote back to this good man and shared that I look at all the testing that comes my way as evidence that I am bothering somebody in the kingdom of darkness. Getting souls saved, baptizing converts, seeing lives transformed, and building and growing a church bothers the Devil. When the kingdom of darkness is being threatened, then the Devil begins bothering us. But, I have already read the last chapter! The kingdom of darkness loses!

I love that song, "I'm on the Winning Side." Christians must not look at testing as, "What is God doing to me?" God is saying, "You and I are giving the Devil a well-deserved bloody lip!" I expect testings and difficulties to come. We will have a lot of affliction if we give the Devil a hard time.

I would hate not to be a threat to the Devil. I have the Holy Ghost protecting me, and greater is He that is in me than he that is in the world! I have the armor of the Lord—the shield of faith and the sword—with which to do battle with the Devil. I have the promises of God!

4. Sorrow is aborted when we let the judgments of others defeat our spirit. Stop chasing the rumors of others and go on living! Don't let that defeat your spirit.

I say, "PBPWMGNFWMY." ("Please be patient with me; God's not finished with me yet.") God is investing in you, and when you go through a tough time, that is the Holy God investing in you and your family. Sorrow is a divine act from the hand of an Almighty God; we must take the sorrow and turn it into joy.

When my wife was expecting, she and I had to attend some special birthing classes where we learned the proper techniques of breathing and how to have focal points to aid in the birthing process. Those classes were not my cup of tea! The day we were on the way to the hospital, we stopped at her parents' house to announce our destination. Basically we nonchalantly made our way to the hospital expecting our first baby. Things progressed so smoothly and nice until about four o'clock in the morning. Suddenly both doctors and nurses seemed to lose all semblance of orderliness as I heard someone scream, "She is going to die; she is going to die; she is going to die!"

When I got someone's attention, I asked, "Who is going to die?"

"Your wife!" I almost totally lost control as I watched them insert IVs into her arm and tried to make her sign papers when she was totally unable to sign anything. I grabbed her hand and scribbled her name on the necessary papers for her. "What is wrong?" I asked.

"The umbilical cord is wrapped twice around the baby's neck. The baby's heartbeat went from 165 beats to 11 beats a minute. Your wife's heartbeat has escalated from 85 beats to 225 beats a minute."

Almost before I heard the explanation, I was ushered from the birthing room. I was in a state of near panic, and immediately I called Brother Hyles on the first phone I found. Since it was just past four o'clock in the morning, he answered with a groggy voice. The moment I heard his voice, I choked out, "Brother Hyles," and that was all I could say.

"Something wrong?"

I could not answer his question. All I could do was weep uncontrollably.

He was at my side in about ten minutes. Relief washed over me as I saw him jogging down the hospital corridor in St. Margaret Hospital. He put his arm around me and said, "It is going to be okay." Tears flooded his eyes as he thought about his baby girl experiencing serious problems.

When I was finally allowed in the room with my wife, a nurse came in and asked, "Daddy, would you like to hold your little girl?" All the hours of frightening sorrow vanished as I took that precious little bundle in my hands. As I looked at Jaclynn's beautiful little face and her perfectly formed little fingers and toes, somehow all the sorrow was gone. Sorrow had become incredible, indescribable joy.

"Sing away sorrow; cast away care." –George W. Bush

Be patient with your sorrow; let it go to full term. Don't rush it, but when it is time to deliver it, give birth to your sorrow. Don't hang on and hang on. Step into the next phase of life. I cannot know what sorrows God will choose to allow into your life. I do know we can tell Him, "Lord, thank You for the sorrow that is a seed that will bring forth joy." We must trust the Miracle Worker Who can turn a bitter pill of sorrow into a glorious child of joy!

"Slow and steady wins the race."
The Hare and the Tortoise
— Robert Lloyd

6

Setting Joy Before You

Suggested Reading:
Hebrews 12:1, 2, 12-15

According to Hebrews 12:1 and 2, every Christian has a race to run. *"…let us run with patience the race that is set before us."* We are not given an option about running this race called the Christian life. This race has every kind of pitfall, every kind of trial, and every kind of accident waiting to happen to the runner.

A Christian survives his race in life by using the formula that Jesus gave in Hebrews 12. Jesus was also running His race, and in His race was a cross. For Him, that cross was, of course, despicable and despised, a shameful humilia-

"If it has to
choose who will
be crucified, the
crowd will always
save Barabbas."
–Jean Cocteau

tion when He was undeservedly stripped naked and punished by people who spat on His face, who whipped Him, and who treated Him shamefully. His captors tried to humiliate and embarrass Him in front of His followers and those who loved Him. They shamefully treated Him, nailed Him to a cross, taunted Him, blasphemed His name, and ultimately murdered Him.

That cross was a necessary part of Jesus' race. The book of Hebrews explains how He survived that race. Jesus ran His race by setting something before Him that brought a little respite—a little relief from the cross. The Bible says that He set joy before Him.

His earthly race began with His birth in Bethlehem in less-than-the-best circumstances. He was born in the privacy of a stall of a displaced farm animal instead of in a hospital. He was placed in a manger instead of in a bed. Within just a couple of years, Herod was calling for His death. Silent years followed. He experienced a little peak at 12 years of age when He was almost a teenager and answered the learned men in the Temple. Then 18 more silent years passed. When Jesus reached 30 years of age, His life was filled with incredible peaks and valleys. His first sermon in His home church would have been called a disaster by many. The townspeople were so upset over His message, they dragged Him outside of the town in an attempt to murder Him by throwing Him over a cliff.

However, some great revivals in some cities followed his ignominious beginning with hundreds being healed of physical ailments. Then He faced times of being mocked by the critics, then times of great blessings, and then times of facing humiliation by critics. More great times of preaching to the multitudes followed. He fed the five thousand. He walked on the water, but then He had to face the doubt of His own disciples and followers. Then came great periods of blessing. Then His forerunner, John the Baptist, who was in jail, asked, "Are you really the One Whom I was proclaiming as the Son of God?"

How that questioning attitude must have devastated the Son of God! Jesus continuously experienced the ups and downs of life until finally the cross loomed into His view. As He faced the obstacles with the shadow of the cross in the future, he planted some joy on the other side of the obstacles and problems He would have to face. Every time Jesus suspected a great trial was threatening on the horizon, He set some joy before Him so He could patiently endure the tribulation.

Each of us is running our individual race. We must set some

joy at strategic places in our race, or according to Hebrews 12:15, we will arrive at the finish line a bitter person. Every person faces about the same amount of negative input in his life. My predecessor, Brother Hyles, taught that if we were to place all the negative things that happen to us in our life on one side of a balance and all the positive things on the other side, the nega-

tives and positives would more than likely balance each other.

Seasons with more difficult times will surely come, but seasons of better times will also come in the race of life. When we go through the seasons of good times, we must learn how to use them so when the rough times come, we can survive. However, the person who does not learn that principle often becomes a very bitter person. I know some people in their thirties who are more bitter than any 75-year-old person I have ever met. On the other hand, I know some 75-year-old people who are delightful because they have learned to properly place some joy in their path.

Running our race is much like running a marathon. A good marathon runner takes about 2fi hours to run 26.2 miles. I person-ally find the history of the marathon fascinating. Its origin is in the Persian Empire, which of course is mentioned in the Bible. In 546 B.C., the Persian Empire extended from Asia to Egypt to what is modern-day Turkey. As the empire strengthened itself from with-in, Darius set his sights on Europe. The Persians landed a large force 26 miles from Athens, Greece, on the plains of Marathon and prepared to attack Greece's largest and most prosperous city state. The Athenians knew they desperately needed the help of Sparta, another city-state with a regimented society built around the art of war.

The Athenian generals sent Phidippides, a professional runner and soldier, to Sparta to ask for help. Phidippides ran the 140-mile, mountainous course from Athens to Sparta in 36 hours. Sparta agreed to help, but "were unable to send it promptly because they did not wish to break their law. It was the ninth day of the month, and they said they could not take the field until the moon was full."[1] Phidippides returned to Athens (another 140 miles) with the disappointing news. Though outnumbered four to one, the Athenians marched to the plains of Marathon to battle the Persians. The defenders mounted a surprise offense which appeared suicidal; however, at the end of the day, 6,400 Persians were dead, and only 192 Athenians had been killed. The Persians who survived fled to their boats and headed south to Athens, hoping to attack the city before the Greek army could reassemble there.

Phidippides, who had fought all morning against the Persians, was once again summoned to run the 26 miles to Athens "to carry both the news of victory and a warning about the approaching Persians."[2]

> Despite his battle fatigue and from running to and from Sparta, Phidippides "rose to the challenge. Pushing himself past normal limits of human endurance, he reached Athens in perhaps three hours, delivered his message, and then died shortly afterward of exhaustion."[3]

With the eventual help of Sparta and some other Greek city-states, the Persians were prevented from conquering Greece.

According to the Greek historian Herodotus, Phidippides did run from Athens to Sparta and back; however, no evidence exists that the runner made the journey from the plains of Marathon to Athens. Still, the run of Phidippides is the stuff from which legends come, and the modern marathon race honors the Grecian's feat of strength and valor. Centuries later in 1896, Michael Bréal petitioned the founder of the first modern Olympic Games being held in Athens, Pierre de Coubertin, to add a marathon race of

24.85 miles. Spiridon "Spiros" Louis, a Greek postal worker from the village of Marusi and veteran of several long military marches, won the race in 2 hours, 58 minutes, and 50 seconds. His average pace was 7:00 minutes per mile!

At the 1908 Olympic Games in London, the marathon distance was changed to 26 miles to cover the ground from Windsor Castle to White City stadium, with 385 yards added on so the race could finish in front of King Edward VII's royal box. The final 26.2 mile distance was established at the 1924 Olympics in Paris as the official marathon distance.[4]

Completing a marathon is often considered to be a superhuman effort. A good training program lasts a minimum of five or six months. The distance run is gradually increased every two weeks. All along the race course, water and light sports drinks are offered to the runners. Water must be consumed regularly to avoid potentially dangerous dehydration. A good runner plans to drink about 4 to 6 ounces of fluids every 15 to 20 minutes. As he passes his relief station, he detours slightly from his path, and without breaking stride, takes the cup of water or sports drink to keep himself hydrated.

Through the years, I have enjoyed watching these elite marathon runners. They are a credit to the "first" runner—Phidippides. On the other hand, I have watched some marathon runners who have obviously not properly planned their water consumption while running. Some consume too much water which leads to hyponatremia[5] which can result in a coma or even death. Runners who make that mistake usually are taken to the hospital where concentrated salt solutions are given intravenously to raise the sodium concentrations in the blood. That runner became overly concerned about becoming dehydrated and drank too much. The other end of the spectrum is a runner who doesn't drink enough water and also has to have IVs and fluids administered to re-hydrate his body.

The Christian who is running his race of life can be likened to a marathon runner. A Christian must also have some water stations and support people to man those stations along his race, or he will dehydrate spiritually. He will become a bitter Christian who blames his acrimony on his circumstances or his supposed mistreatment by others or even God for being unfair. In truth, he did not plan to have the water carriers stationed along his route in life.

I want to run my race, and I want to keep from becoming bitter someday. Therefore, I intend to plan my race and have adequate hydrating stations along my course. As I daily run my race, I can see potential problems looming. Something as simple as a Snickers snack-size candy bar or a Pepsi can help me meet the problem and continue my race. Reading a good biography will give me inspiration and recharge my spirit to help me run my race. I can spend time in prayer and reading God's Word to re-hydrate my dehydrated spirit. Running the race with recharging stations is a little microcosm of what every Christian's life should be.

However, some choose to run their race through life in fear and trepidation. All that is left for them at the end of their race is bitterness and unhappiness. I do not want my life to end in bitterness; spiritually I want to live a sweet life. Every day of my life I plan something I enjoy doing that day. In so doing, I am setting joy before me. My joy might be a Reese's-Peanut-Butter-Cup break. My father-in-law taught me to love Reese's Peanut Butter Cups. I can read a little more in a biography and learn about some great men who have gone through trials and difficulties and successfully ran their race. I do not intend to let the obstacles I encounter on my race to trip me and make me a bitter Christian! Consequently, I am enjoying my race of life because I have set joy before me!

How to Run Your Race Successfully

1. **Place some joy on your path for when you know you will need it.** Most of us reading this book have lived long enough

to understand that some bad days will come into our life. We have had enough Christmases to know how we feel on December 26. We know and understand that an emotional letdown often follows the Christmas holidays. Returning to work after a family vacation often brings an emotional discontentment. If that is the case, we must plan to set some joy on the other side of letdown time, instead of letting it trip us and cause bitterness. Hebrews 12:2, "...who for the joy that was set before him endured the cross, despising the shame...." Jesus endured the cross. With Jesus as our example, we can go through whatever God or the circumstances or the world or the flesh brings, and we can survive it by setting joy in front of us at the correct places.

Thankfully, most of life is quite predictable. For instance, in my schedule, I plan to perform a wedding at First Baptist Church of Hammond about every week from June through November. On June 1, 2001, I planned to walk my daughter down the aisle and give her away in marriage. I began planning to make that walk with her when I brought her home from St. Margaret Hospital in 1981. I planned because my pastor, my very wise father-in-law, Brother Hyles, told me to plan. He taught me to be prepared for what life will bring. I have had the misfortune of watching some parents be unprepared for that wedding day. The father has to force out the words, "Her mother and I do," because he wasn't prepared to make that walk with his daughter. Both parents fall apart and lose control, and for the next five years, they make life miserable for the couple because they did not properly prepare.

I remember the day I said to little Jaclynn, "You sure do love Jesus, don't you?" Just as well as I remember asking that question, I remember her answer: "I love Jesus almost as much as I love you, Daddy!"

I held her close as she tightly hugged my neck. The tears rolled down her little cheeks and joined mine. That little girl snagged my heart, and I loved her more than I loved life itself. But I knew that one day I had to give her up for the right young man!

I knew the day would come when I would walk her down an aisle and place her hand in the arm of her chosen. We had a good time at her wedding as we reminisced, laughed, and shared stories. We had not one sad moment because we had planned joy. We had planned for life beyond her absence from our house.

For instance, we planned to turn Jaclynn's bedroom into our laundry room. Someone asked, "How could you take her bedroom and turn it into a laundry room?"

"It was our plan," I truthfully answered. "We planned to convert that room into a laundry room."

When the hurdle comes of letting go of your children to someone totally unqualified (or so you think), have some joy planned ahead of you. That alone is one good reason a couple should have a good marriage. Always be planning and building a good relationship as a husband and wife so you have some joy beyond the empty nest.

> "Many persons have a wrong idea of what constitutes true happiness. It is not attained through self-gratification but through fidelity to a worthy purpose."
> – Helen Keller

Nearly everyone can list 90 percent of the events that will come in a period of 12 months. For instance, you know if you have a doctor's appointment scheduled. You know in advance if you have to go for surgery. You know if you have a child who will be advancing from one school to another. Of course, you know if you have a child beginning school for the first time. You know if you will be saying, "Goodbye," to a son or daughter going to college. You know if there will be a wedding in the near future. As you see these coming events of life—the hurdles that trip up some people and cause them to fall—don't angrily raise an objection, "God, what are You doing to me?" Meet the hurdle head on, and find the joy that is set before you so you can endure the marathon race of life. Running the race of life need not be so complicated! Just plan to live life happily.

2. Extend the fullness of joy. Brother Hyles taught us there are three phases to every event of life. First is the *anticipation*.

When Brother Hyles had a difficult counseling appointment, he promised himself a Reese's Peanut Butter Cup as a reward. For some reason, that chocolate and peanut butter mixing together made him happy.

Next is *participation*. Was it worth going through that problem to have that Reese's Peanut Butter Cup? To Brother Hyles it was well worth hurdling over another's problem so he could enjoy the joy that he had set for himself ahead of time! He enjoyed and savored the taste of his favorite candy bar.

Lastly, take time for *reflection.*

In everything in life, there should be anticipation, participation, and reflection. For instance, at Christmastime, the family gets together for the Christmas story, the opening of gifts, the traditional family meal, the clean-up, the fun, and the games. After Christmas is over and the gifts have been put away, time should be spent in reflection. "Wasn't that a good time with my family?" "Wasn't that a good meal that Mom prepared?" "Wasn't it good for the family to be all together again?" Reflection is a necessary part of joy. Sad to say, many enjoy only the participation; there is no savoring of the moment. Every joy moment needs to be anticipated, then enjoyed in participation, and finally enjoyed a third time in reflection. Only when all three steps are taken is there fullness of joy.

3. Don't choose joy robbers for your joy. You might say, "I happen to know what makes me feel good. I will use my credit card to go shopping." I call that choice a joy robber. The way you have chosen to meet your obstacle on your race of life often creates an even greater obstacle. After all, when the debt comes due in a month and you have no extra money to pay the bill, you say, "I am going to go shopping to forget my problem." Four or five years later, going through a bankruptcy is not fun. Nobody goes through a bankruptcy saying, "That was fun! Let's do it again!"

Many people choose to entertain all the typical joy robbers of life, namely sinful activities like drinking, smoking, taking recreational drugs, embracing pornography, fornicating, etc. A joy rob-ber opens a door with more problems. I find it interesting that the woman who comes to tell me that she is expecting a baby outside the bonds of matrimony never says, "Brother Schaap, I have good news for you! I am expecting an illegitimate baby!" Of course, not! They are always long-faced, have no prospects for a job, have no place to live, and their question is always, "Can you please help me?" Fornication and the results of fornication do not bring joy; rather, they are joy robbers.

On the race of life, don't place joy robbers along the way. At the end of your life you will inevitably say, "What a miserable waste of life I had."

4. Don't make your joy depend upon what others do for you. Don't place joy in what others may or may not do for you. People are fickle. How unwise to anticipate a salary bonus; one just may not come. We cannot let our joy depend on what some-one else may do for us. That someone might backslide, let us down, or have a financial setback. Your joy should not come only from what people do for you; rather, let your joy come from some-thing much more stable. Carefully and purposefully choose what brings you joy. A person can have joy any time he wants to have joy.

Any time I want to, I can say, "I am feeling a little blue, I am going to have a little joy. I think it is time to just realize how good life is. I am going to have a Reese's Peanut Butter Cup!"

Many people's method of finding joy is too complicated. They believe their joy will come in a big event like a trip to Disney World. You have to be careful that your joy is not based on some-thing so expensive that you must depend on someone else. In all seriousness, for me a Snickers candy bar, a good book to read, a bottle of Pepsi, and some homemade cookies bring me lots of joy!

5. Let your joy be a planned action for someone else. Bake some cookies for the neighbors. Pay for a lunch with a good friend. If you are always expecting your friend to pay, you will leave joyless. Visit a shut-in who lives in a nursing home. Make a visit to the cemetery, and spend time remembering and reflecting on some loved ones who played a vital role in your life. I frequently visit our mausoleum and remember Brother Hyles. My wife and I love to go there and visit the grave of Sharon Stromberg, one of my wife's dearest friends who survived a terrible automobile accident but was taken in a fire close to Christmas day. We visit baby land, look at all the names of the little babies, and remember the families. "Precious memories, how they linger!" Those memories stir me to survive a little longer and to go a little further. I have never left the cemetery depressed when I go there to take a joy break.

6. The less it costs and the more it benefits someone else, the greater the joy. A homemade card from a child is much more enjoyable to me than one bought in a store. I savor the time, the thoughtfulness, and the love behind the card. The card probably cost practically nothing, but the joy of both the giver and the receiver is heightened by the time, the thought, and the effort put forth. Time is life.

Every day of my life I plan something that I know will bring me joy. For instance, I like to fill my bird feeders and watch the birds flock to them. I have a birding book, and I like to try to identify the different birds I see and enjoy. When I am really stressed and feel I cannot go another step, I shut the door, turn off the lights, put a towel on the floor, lie down, and talk to God. Thirty minutes with God brings joy.

My father-in-law, Brother Hyles, would buy a newspaper and a Diet Dr. Pepper. Drinking that Diet Dr. Pepper and reading the newspaper constituted his joy moment for the day.

- A wife can plan a special meal for her family or her husband.
- Go for a walk with your wife.
- Schedule a half hour to talk to God in a quiet place.
- Play a game with the family.

- Light a fire in the fireplace.
- Play a musical instrument.

I would never play my saxophone publicly, but sometimes I get it out and play for half an hour for me. I have never put away that instrument without feeling good. These are joy moments.

7. You can find your joy in looking to Jesus. When Jesus was going through the toughest time in His life, He found his joy in thinking about mankind. He thought about you and me! He saw what His sacrifice on Calvary would do for mankind, and He said, "I think I can make it."

"Oh, the fullness, pleasure, sheer excitement of knowing God on earth!"
–Jim Elliot

If Christ's looking at us gave Him joy to endure Calvary, then we can look at Him and find joy in our deepest crisis. I have found that even through the deepest crisis, if I just look to Jesus, the Author and Finisher of my faith, all those problems are nothing when I have my eyes on Jesus.

There is not one problem in this world that cannot be solved by Christ Jesus. However, on our race of life, we are not trying to solve all the problems. We run our race effectively by planting joy ahead of time along that race of life.

*"We should all do what in the long run
gives us joy, even if it is only picking
grapes or sorting the laundry."*
                                    –E. B. White

7

The Joy Robbers

Suggested Reading:
James 1:1-8

T he book of James is such an intensely practical book. James
addresses the issues right where we live. The words "joy" and
"rejoicing" are found several times in the book of James, and he
explains very concretely and very simply why some Christians
have joy and why others do not have joy.

As I stated in chapter one, a person chooses whether or not
he wants to be a positive, rejoicing Christian.
To rejoice is a choice, or, a person chooses to be
a pessimistic, bitter, old saint. That choice is
what I call an indirect choice. Let me explain.
A person doesn't just say, "I believe I'll have joy
today," and start acting happy. A person doesn't
just start singing, "I've got the joy, joy, joy, joy
down in my heart," and suddenly say, "Guess
what? I chose joy, and now I am full of it!" I
hate to disappoint the person who believes

> " Joy increases as
> you give it and
> diminishes as you
> try to keep it for
> yourself. In giving,
> it will accumulate
> a deposit of joy
> greater than you
> ever believed
> possible."
> –Norman Vincent
> Peale

that, but the truth is, he is not full of joy! Joy is not simply choosing a word and possessing it.

Rather, you choose joy by choosing that which gives you joy.
Let me share an illustration. When I got married, I weighed 142

pounds, and I wanted to gain some weight. (From the time I was about 17 years of age until the age of 38, I weighed 142 pounds.) Consequently, I told my new bride that I wanted to gain some weight, so she promptly put me on a "diet" of 8,000 calories a day. I *lost* three pounds! Since I really wanted to gain some weight and my diet wasn't working, I began to study how to gain weight. The obvious solution—eating more food and increasing my caloric intake wasn't working for me. I soon learned that a weight-lifting program would help a person gain weight. Truthfully, weight lifting did not sound good to me. I had carried my share of cement blocks when I worked for my dad, but I did remember gaining weight. (In fact, that was when I went from 115 pounds to the 142 pounds I had weighed for 21 years.)

> There are four keys to gaining muscular bodyweight: adequate caloric intake, adequate intake of protein, a training stimulus sufficient to stimulate growth (exercise), and avoiding activities that tear down the body. In order to gain weight, more calories must be taken in than the person expends. Calories an be increased by consuming a greater quantity of foods (my wife's plan). People who are trying to gain weight may need to eat in a way that would not be encouraged for the average person. This is not a license to eat candy bars and donuts all day! Complete proteins are the building blocks for muscle tissue and particular attention must be paid to getting adequate protein when trying to gain weight. Exercise creates the demand for muscle tissue and food supplies the needed material. The one who is working to gain weight should minimize the stress of life and get plenty of rest.[1]

Still, even realizing that I could gain weight by lifting did not make me want to choose that method. Weight lifting takes time, and besides, it still sounded boring to me!

In spite of my negative attitude, I bought a bench, an Olympic bar, some weights, and began my program of weight lifting. My

The Joy Robbers | 89

plan wasn't to gain big muscles; I just lifted to gain weight, and it wasn't long until I had gained 20 pounds! Weight lifting indeed gave me the results that I wanted—additional weight—but also I found that my health improved because of the lifting. I chose a procedure that gave me the desired end result. I could not choose to gain weight; I could only choose that which would make me gain weight.

In the same way, we cannot just choose joy; we must choose that which will bring us joy. Unfortunately, some of what brings joy are not the choices the average person would want to make. That is exactly why so many people miss joy—that which gives joy is not always as attractive as that which does not give joy. In fact, sometimes those activities which look the most pleasing actually are the biggest joy robbers in life. Joy is the by-product of making good choices. For example, I have a happy marriage; however, my happy marriage is not because I chose a happy marriage. I married well, and that well-chosen selection gave me the joy or happy marriage for which I was looking.

> "Desire joy and thank God for it. Renounce it, if need be, for other's sake. That's joy beyond joy."
> –Robert Browning

Saying, "I want to have a happy home," will not automatically result in a happy home. A magician doesn't magically appear with his wand, wave it, and presto, a happy home appears! No! You choose that which produces a happy home. Sad to say, some people who really want to make the correct choices, instead choose what I call joy robbers.

Some choose a joy robber called an adulterous affair instead of choosing a faithful marriage. I have counseled with scores of people involved in adulterous affairs, and I have yet to have anyone come to my office with joy on his face to tell me that he is living in adultery. When I tell that person's spouse, "I have the unfortunate task of telling you that your spouse has been living in adultery," that person doesn't say, "Praise God. I've got the joy, joy,

joy...." Of course, that is not the response of a heartbroken spouse. There is no joyfulness in this joy robber! The guilty person may have been seeking another source of joy, but he soon found his joy was a robber. He then lost his joy in that which he thought would give him joy. *"The thief cometh not, but for to steal, and to kill, and to destroy...."* (John 10:10) Adultery is a joy robber that destroys relationships. People become involved with a joy robber thinking it will bring happiness and joy, but in reality, it does not bring anything but unhappiness and a lack of joy.

"**H**appiness is not a reward—it is a consequence. Suffering is not a punishment— it is a result." –Robert Green Ingersoll

Some very unhappy Christians consider their personal sorrow to be a tribulation from God (or a persecution from Satan) when in truth, their sorrow is the by-product of choosing joy robbers rather than joy givers. An emotional thief has come into the lives of these people and has stolen their mind and heart and has replaced joy with sadness. That person did not purposely choose to be unhappy. Rather, he chose something that brought unhappiness; he chose a joy robber.

Often what looks like happiness actually brings the opposite of happiness. Generally, Christians are not unhappy because they want to be unhappy. They are unhappy because they repeatedly choose what they erroneously believe will bring them joy but does not. They then lose their joy because they do not recognize that which will give them joy. Joy is always a by-product of another decision.

James 1:2 says, *"My brethren, count it all joy when ye fall into divers temptations."* When I read that verse, it doesn't sound like a pleasurable source of joy. *Divers* means "a variety of kinds," and the word *temptation* means "a testing of faith." The proof of the proper place to find joy is in the following verse. *"Knowing this, that the trying of your faith worketh patience."* The temptation is a trying or a proving of what I believe, and God allows me to go through incredible proofs or spiritually speaking, "final exams."

We are daily tested repeatedly and constantly by the world and the flesh and the Devil. That temptation might be a medical condition or a financial condition or a relationship being sorely tested.

"Maturity is: the ability to stick with a job until it's finished; the ability to do a job without being supervised; the ability to carry money without spending it; and the ability to bear an injustice without wanting to get even."
– Abigail Van Buren

When we are being tested, God wants us to understand that the trying of our faith can be one of the greatest joy givers in our life. James 1:2 says, "...count it all joy...." The word *count* in that verse is used like a military term—"to set in order in your mind" or "to march in cadence." James was saying that we are marching into joy by having our faith tested. "Hup, two, three, four, testing brings joy!"

In the first four verses of James, the Bible explains what testing (temptation) brings. The Bible says the testing or trial of your faith brings patience, and patience brings maturity. *"Knowing this, that the trying of your faith worketh patience. But let patience have her perfect work, that ye may be perfect and entire, wanting nothing."* (James 1:3, 4) The phrase *"perfect and entire, wanting nothing"* means "a complete, mature individual."

When a person grows to his full stature from babyhood, not only does he have all of his fingers and toes, but his fingers and toes have also grown in the proper proportion. An adult is at the fullest height he will ever be; I am at the fullest height I will ever be. In fact, I am going to start going the other direction—get-

"Maturity is achieved when a person postpones immediate pleasures for long-term values."
–Joshua Loth Leibman

ting shorter and shorter! According to this Bible definition of mature, I am perfect and entire in the sense that I have all the parts that I am supposed to have, and all my parts are at their maximum adulthood right now. My mind is probably the best it will ever be. I have reached full maturity. In the Christian life, testing brings patience, and patience brings maturity.

> "Maturity is that time when the mirrors in our mind turn to windows, and instead of seeing the reflection of ourselves, we see others."
> – Author Unknown

James 1:9 and 10 tells what maturity brings. *"Let the brother of low degree rejoice in that he is exalted: But the rich, in that he is made low: because as the flower of the grass he shall pass away."* This verse is teaching that as a Christian goes through life's testings, he comes to the realization what ultimately produces stability in his life. Tests bring patience; patience brings maturity, and maturity brings stability. It does not matter what the Christian's external condition is if he is stable internally.

Some people say, "If I had a little more money, I could be more stable."

Money does not bring stability. The great secret about money that people fail to understand is that money brings great instability. On the average, poor people are much more stable than rich people. People with money know that it is very difficult to handle money properly. Probably the most difficult thing for me to handle is the wisdom God gives a pastor. The Bible says in Ecclesiastes to be careful how much wisdom you seek because it can create a tremendous problem—much like wealth does. Solomon mishandled his God-given wisdom, and all kinds of trouble invaded his life. Wisdom, money, power, and authority—all the things that people believe will give them stability—often bring great instability.

I was listening to an interview of a lady who makes $200,000,000 dollars a year. That is pretty good money; it's definitely more than I make! She said, "I have been poor, and I have been rich. I enjoy being rich more than being poor. However, several problems come with having money. I don't know who my friends are. I don't trust my family. Everybody likes me because of what I can do for them. I have to make so many decisions that it just absolutely stresses my mind."

We think, "I'd like to have that kind of stress!" You believe you would like to have it until you get it.

According to James 1:9, I should rejoice when I have stability because stability brings joy, and joy comes from stability. Stability comes from maturity. Maturity comes from patience. Patience comes by being tested. So if I choose joy, I am asking God to give me testing.

So I say, "God, I want to have joy!"

God says, "Problems, problems."

The average Christian rebels, "I don't want problems! Keep the stupid problems away from me!"

God says, "I thought you wanted joy?"

1. I lose joy when I do not understand the purpose of the test of my faith. Joy only comes from testing, and testing brings patience, and patience gives you maturity, and maturity gives you stability, and stability is joy! That is God's formula for having joy.

"If you want joy, real joy, wonderful joy," let God test your faith! Enduring and bearing the testing will bring maturity, and maturity says, "...for I know whom I have believed...." Maturity says, "And though after my skin worms destroy this body, yet in my flesh shall I see God." (Job 19:26)

> "My faith has found a resting place
> Not in device nor creed;
> I trust the Ever-living One,
> His wounds for me shall plead."

Maturity places his confidence in the Word of God.

However, when testing comes into the life of some Christians, they choose an exit instead of bearing the test. James 1:12 says, "Blessed is the man that endureth temptation...." The word endure means "he stays under it." He doesn't find an exit or quit because he understands the truth that testing brings patience, patience brings maturity, maturity brings stability, and stability brings joy.

"Blessed is the man that endureth temptation: for when he is tried, he shall receive the crown of life, which the Lord hath promised to them *that love him. Let no man say when he is tempted, I am tempted of God: for God cannot be tempted with evil, neither tempteth he any man: But every man is tempted, when he is drawn away of his own lust, and enticed. Then when lust hath conceived, it bringeth forth sin: and sin, when it is finished, bringeth forth death. Do not err, my beloved brethren.*" (James 1:12-16) Sometimes when a Christian's faith is tested, he bails out and chooses an alternate way out of the situation.

Suppose a person's marriage is being tested. Rather than enduring the testing and finding joy, the out of an adulterous affair is chosen. When that marriage breaks apart, nobody has joy in the divorce court or in a custody battle. Suppose a person's finances are being tested. Instead of enduring the test, the out of gambling is chosen. Nobody will have joy when the home is repossessed and your loved ones and all your belongings are sitting in the front yard. Passing the test is so much better than crying yourself to sleep at night and feeling like you live in hell on earth. These kinds of choices are joy robbers.

2. I lose my joy when I blame my sins on the testing or on God. Since some do not understand the purpose of trials, they go into sin, find that they have chosen a joy robber, and then blame God when they get into trouble. It is not God's fault when we bail out on Him! God does not tempt the Christian with evil; He tests his faith, and if the Christian stands under the testing and does not run into sin, then the testing will ultimately bring joy. Once the test is successfully passed and joy comes, the Christian is then ready for the next test because he wants more joy. When a Christian is being tested, he can count it all joy because it means that joy is just down the road; joy is coming in the morning.

Failure to recognize the correct steps to joy will cause some to err and to find a substitute that they think will bring joy. Not one of these substitutes—cigarettes, drugs, liquor—will bring joy. Instead, they will steal your money, your marriage, your children, and your soul. There is no joy in a hangover or wasteful living. No joy is the result of a one-night stand. There is no joy in any substitutes at all. Why is there no joy? You were being tested by God, and you bailed out. He was trying to give you what you wanted—joy—and you chose an artificial joy robber.

3. I lose my joy when I act on anger rather than obedience. James says testing will lead to joy...with a few steps in between. Being tested today does not mean having joy tomorrow! Anger comes when you refuse to let a trial that was ordained of God bring you further maturity.

Some Christians are like little children—kicking and screaming and wanting their own way. God probably says, "Just one good cuff across the back of the head will take care of the problem." Slowing down the testing process and refusing to move forward retards the Christian's growth. In other words, he is spiritually challenged and is robbing himself of joy.

In a period of two weeks, I had no less than 17 angry families in my office. Dating couples were drawing their parents into some vicious conflicts. Some of these families had actually gotten into physical fights. Parents had actually taken whips to their adult children, and some adult children called the police. Why? These family members had chosen wrath instead of obedience. No good can ever come from anger.

> "Anybody can become angry—that is easy; but to be angry with the right person, and to the right degree, and at the right time, and for the right purpose, and in the right way—that is not within everybody's power and is not easy."
> –Aristotle

James 1:17, "*Every good gift and every perfect gift is from above, and cometh down from the Father of lights, with whom is no variableness, neither shadow of turning.*" According to this verse, everything good we receive is by the hand of God. If we cannot trust God, we will resort to every kind of devious, devilish behavior in order to get our way.

I can think of only superlatives to describe four of the seventeen families—outstanding, excellent Christians. They came seeking counseling because they knew they needed wisdom, they

> "Anger is a momentary madness, so control your passion or it will control you."
> –Horace

wanted to do right, they wanted to obey God, and I believe He will bless them mightily because of their humble hearts. Thirteen of the families refused to come back for further counseling because they believed they knew what was best. To them, angry words are better, fist fights are better, and even jail is better.

James 1:19 and 20 say, *"Wherefore, my beloved brethren, let every man be swift to hear, slow to speak, slow to wrath: For the wrath of man worketh not the righteousness of God."* Cursing, anger, and rebellion toward parents will never bring joy. A person does not get joy by choosing the wrath of man. When we do not exercise control, we will not have joy.

Having a bitter heart and an angry spirit is so contrary to the victory that Jesus promises. How dwelleth the love of God in us? The only language that will bring joy is, "Whatever You want, God!"

I understand the situations that arise when children reach dating age. Our daughter, Jaclynn, dated many young men before she met Mr. Right. I think her attraction to men all began when she fell in love with the doctor who delivered her! She liked boys in grade school. She liked them in junior high school, and she liked them in high school. She was very proper about her dating, and my wife and I never had one moment of difficulty with any boy or family of a boy she dated. In fact, when a dating relationship ended, our families remained friends. I always understood that children grow up. As they mature, they feel love, and their love is very real. Because these are normal relationships, we did not discourage Jaclynn in her dating.

My daughter would come home and say, "Dad, I am dating so-and-so."

"I know," I would answer.

"I think another girl likes him. What do I do about it?"

"Nothin'. Just relax."

"But Dad, what if she likes him? What if he likes her!?"

"If he likes her, then he is not the one for you," I truthfully answered. "If a guy is not sold on you, you don't want him."

I was very much the opposite of my daughter. I did not date until I went to college in Minnesota, and a girl asked me out for the first date! It was not that I did not want to date. It just so happens that I attended a church with 45 people, and the girls there were my cousins! As I watched our daughter date, I couldn't help but think, "Whose genes does she have?" I decided she had her mother's genes because I had to wait for her mother to stop dating two guys so I could move in!

Jaclynn dated and dated and dated. However, I married the fourth girl I dated. That was my extensive dating life. My point in sharing these illustrations is that young people will like each other. So why don't parents and children just agree to get along with each other? Being so wrapped up in your children's dating life that it makes you emotionally hot means that you are too close to the situation. Parents are supposed to be stable, and stability brings joy.

Grown children have to go through the tests of their faith to see if they can trust God enough to give them His choice. Parents have to let their young people alone to be tested. If you are causing strife between the person you are dating and his/her parents, you are not the will of God for him/her. You might be later on in life, but not until you learn stability from being tested. Wanting your own way and doing whatever is necessary to have your own way is childish immaturity.

When I was engaged to my wife, a young man came to Hyles-Anderson College for his master's degree. He made it a point to let me know why he came to college. "I came to marry Cindy Hyles," he boldly announced.

"That is going to be tough," I returned.

"Why?"

"I am engaged to her," I said.

"I don't care! I am going to take her from you," he warned.

I shook hands with him and said, "God bless you."

I did not dislike that young man then, and I don't dislike him now. His announcement did not bother me in the slightest. When I told my fiancée, she asked, "How do you feel about that?"

"I know that you are smart enough to recognize a good thing when you've got one," I answered. "I believe I am dating an intelligent woman."

"If you weren't so proud and arrogant," she bantered, "I would say you are right!"

Truthfully, I was never scared about losing her. I knew how to get her, and I know how to keep her.

I love the members of the 17 angry families who came to my office. Because I love them, I told them they had no business letting anger take their joy. No one had any business calling the police, fist fighting, or using God's name in vain. *"For the wrath of man worketh not the righteousness of God."* (James 1:20) Those who resort to wrath are unstable people who have not gathered the maturity that comes from the patience from having their faith tested. Anger is a joy robber.

Attacks are constantly launched against First Baptist Church of Hammond. A good preacher friend of mine said, "Do you realize there is a major attack against you personally?" When I answered yes, he said, "Somebody really doesn't like you."

I was reminded of the little ditty Brother Hyles used to sing, "Sometimes I'm happy, sometimes I'm blue, my disposition depends on you." Then he would add, "That is not the truth. My disposition does not depend upon you." I learned the truth behind that little ditty; my disposition and my joy are not dependent upon anyone's being happy or sad with me.

4. I lose my joy when I choose to err from the faith. A Christian says, "I have had enough of this testing; I am going to go the easy way." He walks away from all that God has to offer and chooses instead a life of sin. It might seem to be more fun to watch a movie or to drink an alcoholic beverage or to smoke cigarettes or to look at some pornography or to waste money in frivolity. However, God says enjoying *the pleasures of sin for a season* will not bring joy. Erring from the faith and choosing sin is a joy robber.

God blesses those who come through the test. The tests will come to our lives—whether they be medical tests, financial tests, or difficult family tests.

When you try to get away from that testing and declare, "I am not going to be tested," you are choosing a joy robber. When your faith is tested, count it all joy. Eventually, you will have great joy, and the happiest people are tested people. Testing brings patience which brings maturity which brings stability which brings joy. Choosing that which gives me joy will bring me joy.

> "He that can have patience can have what he will."
> –Benjamin Franklin

"Among the attributes of God, although they are all equal, mercy shines with even more brilliancy than justice."
—Cervantes

8

Mercy Rejoiceth Against Judgment

Suggested Reading:
James 2:1-13

The Old Testament account of Joseph and his brothers is the backdrop for the truth presented in this chapter. The phrase *"...mercy rejoiceth against judgment..."* beautifully defines the life of Joseph. I have often wondered if the attitudes Joseph developed made him one of the great saints in the Old Testament. More than likely his attitudes were impressed firmly in his mind as a reaction from the mistreatment he received by his very arrogant and envious brothers. During Joseph's teenage years, he was the youngest of the brothers; and at that time, he was terribly mistreated by them.

"Sweet mercy is nobility's true badge."
—William Shakespeare

Joseph dreamed a dream that his brothers did not like, so they conspired to murder their brother, who was also the favored son. The brothers intended to fabricate some lie about his demise. However, his older brother Reuben, intervened and persuaded them instead to sell Joseph to some Midianite merchants. He argued they could be rid of him without resorting to murder. The brothers believed the sale of Joseph would free them forever of their hated baby brother.

Joseph was taken to Egypt where he was sold to a powerful bureaucrat in the Egyptian dynasty named Potiphar. Joseph excelled in his work and consequently became a very trusted man in the household of Potiphar. However, Mrs. Potiphar, a conspiring woman with adulterous eyes looked at Joseph and tried to seduce him into committing adultery. Joseph maintained his integrity and his moral character and repeatedly declined her offers. Finally, he had to physically flee from her advances. *"And she caught him by his garment, saying, Lie with me: and he left his garment in her hand, and fled, and got him out."* (Genesis 39:12) Feeling totally scorned and rejected, she became angry, and in an act of vengeance she called for the other men of the house to rescue her and showed them her evidence of Joseph's attempted rape. When Potiphar came home, she repeated her story and showed him the garment she had managed to take from Joseph as he fled from her. I personally do not believe that Potiphar believed his scheming wife, but he had to live with her, so he took her side and ordered Joseph to be sent to prison for his crime that was not a crime.

While in prison for at least a minimum of two years and probably much longer, Joseph's wrists or ankles or both were in irons. Even though he was much mistreated, he excelled in his attitude and became a trusted man to his own prison keeper. *"But the LORD was with Joseph, and shewed him mercy, and gave him favour in the sight of the keeper of the prison."* (Genesis 39:21)

No doubt Joseph had plenty of time to consider the abandonment of his family, his mistreatment and betrayal at the hand of his brothers, and their merchandising him into slavery. What a forgotten feeling he must have had knowing that his father believed him dead. More than likely, he believed that he would never be rescued, he would die a slave in a foreign country, and not one person would ever know the truth of what had really transpired. While Joseph was sitting alone and forgotten in that prison, I am quite certain he had many hundreds of hours to think through what course of action he would take—should the opportunity ever afford itself.

Should he conspire? Should he try to plan an escape to go back home, reveal the incredible dastardly deeds of his brothers' conspiracy, and exercise vengeance on his brothers? Or, should he accept his situation as somehow being a divine act and that maybe God has more noble plans for him? Should he see his unjust incarceration as God's using the mischief of others to perform an even greater deed of service? His youthful dreams of becoming the family patriarch even though he was one of the youngest brothers, the ruler of the nation of Israel, and of his brothers bowing before him were foolishness and would never come to pass.

- "What choice do I make?"
- "Do I choose bitterness and vengeance or do I choose to exercise faith and mercy?"
- "Do I decide that one day I will get even with my brothers for their unfounded, unwarranted, unjustified, unprovoked, uncalled-for hatred and exercise vengeance against them?
- Do I exercise wisdom and faith and mercy and grace and a higher nobler trust in God Who says that this evil can be meant for good if I have confidence in Him?
- What choice do I make?

Because we have the inspired Word of God to read the final chapter about Joseph's life, we have the luxury of knowing the full story. It is not difficult for us to say, "Joseph, choose faith! Take the side of mercy! Joseph, your dream will become a reality!" God, Who always knows the end from the beginning, **always** encourages choosing mercy over judgment because mercy will always rejoice against judgment.

Choosing to show mercy is always the choice that brings joy—judgment does not. To exercise vindication, vengeance, and a get-even mentality is not to choose joy; it is to choose strife, wrath, unhappiness, and the absence of joy because *"...the wrath of man worketh not the righteousness of God."* (James 1:20) To exercise an uncontrolled temper, to exercise anger, or to get even with someone who has hurt you is to take the place of God. God said, *"...Vengeance is mine; I will repay, saith the Lord."* (Romans 12:19)

Choose mercy even though they may believe that mercy is not called for, not warranted, and not justified, for that is what mercy means.

- *Mercy* says, "I am going to choose a course that is illogical with the course you have chosen."
- *Mercy* says, "I have chosen joy in the presence of your evil conspiracy."
- *Mercy* says, "I will choose my personal joy rather than get even with you which is what my flesh would warrant and justify."
- *Mercy* says, "I will seize the right course of action."

To many, the right course of action always seems to be to get even and to balance the scales of justice; however, mercy always rejoices over judgment. Choosing mercy is choosing joy. Choosing judgment is choosing the absence of joy.

"Happiness is not a destination. It is a method of life."
–Burton Hillis

Choosing judgment is choosing fear, torment, strife, envy, and every evil way. Choosing judgment means passing on to succeeding generations a mentality like the famous Hatfield and McCoy feud. Many people unaware of the fact that there really were two families named the Hatfields and the McCoys who feuded off and on for nearly 30 years. Theirs was not just a terrible, tragic quarrel between two proud backwoods families. Rather, their strife boiled into a dispute involving two states which ultimately ended in a United States Supreme decision about the extradition of prisoners from state to state.

The Tug Fork River sliced between West Virginia and Kentucky in a craggy mountain terrain. The river also became the line of demarcation for the Hatfields of Logan County, West Virginia, and Kentucky's Pike County where the McCoys lived. The independent-minded states would face a great challenge with the coming of the Civil War when men from both states died for both the Union and the South. If not for the war and the divisions it created, the tragedy of the Hatfields and the McCoys might never have been.

Before the Civil War, a quiet unity dominated the strong mountain people. Hatfields married McCoys, and all was well with the clans. Family patriarchs led the family factions. In Kentucky, Randolph (Ol' Ran'l) McCoy was the undisputed leader, a man about whom others said seldom laughed. A former Confederate officer, Captain William Anderson (Devil Anse) Hatfield, who ruled the clan in West Virginia, was a legend in his own time because of his incredible marksmanship and his sense of humor. The distance between the two men's cabins was roughly eight miles.

When West Virginia was admitted to the Union in 1863, Devil Anse Hatfield who was a Southern sympathizer, became acutely aware that he and his people lived in danger. In the name of defending his home, Devil Anse formed the Logan Wildcats, which became one of the most feared guerrilla bands. The Hatfields too often forgot their commendable objective of defending their homes and began capitalizing on less-than-honorable spoils of war. In a getting-even and a paying-back aggressiveness, guerrillas from both the Hatfields and the McCoys stole hogs, horses, and hides. The two mountain families took turns being victims and attackers. The clans' anger toward one another increasingly grew hotter until finally on January 7, 1865, the first victim of the feud was claimed. Randolph McCoy's younger brother, Asa Harmon McCoy, who was injured while fighting for the Union, was discharged and on his way home when two of the Hatfields found him and killed him. The case against the killers of Harmon McCoy ended with no suspect brought to trial.

With time's passing, Hatfields and McCoys forgot the tensions of the Civil War for 13 years. The families again intermarried. However, one day in 1878, the McCoy patriarch stopped to visit Floyd Hatfield, his wife's brother-in-law. While there, Randolph spotted a familiar-looking pig, and he accused Floyd of stealing. (In those days, the ears of the pigs were notched for ownership, and the pigs were allowed to run free until herding time.) "The common bond that existed between him and Hatfield because of their marriage to sisters was shattered."[1] When the two took the dispute to court, Bill Staton, a brother-in-law of Ellison Hatfield, swore that Floyd Hatfield was the owner of the hog. "Randolph McCoy accused Staton of swearing to a lie and hurled a rock at him."[2]

Staton's declaration marked him for death which he found at the hands of Paris and Sam McCoy, nephews of the clan leader. When Sam McCoy was tried for the murder of Staton in a court of law, Devil Anse intervened and instructed the jurors to acquit Sam. As a result of Sam's trial, an even greater hatred burned within the McCoys for the ignominy they suffered at Hatfield hands.

Probably the match that lit the fuse to the powder keg was Rose Anne McCoy, a daughter of Randolph, falling in love with Johnson (Johnse) Hatfield, a son of Devil Anse. Rose Anne inevitably became a casualty of the mountain war. "Fate had been against the love of Johnse and Rose Anne from the beginning."[3] When the McCoys marked Johnse for death and captured him, Rose Anne rode to her father, Devil Anse, who gathered the clan, cut off the McCoys, and reclaimed his son. The powder keg blew, and "the night of August 9, 1882, was etched for life in the memories of the mountaineers along Tug Fork."[4]

Ellison Hatfield soon died at the hand of the McCoys and in retaliation, three McCoy brothers were systematically slaughtered.

Tug Fork had never been as sheerly the dividing line between West Virginia and Kentucky as on the morning of August 10, 1882. What had taken place was a formal declaration of war. There could be no peace now between Hatfields and McCoys.[5]

The two clans began systematically ambushing, attacking, and killing each other with little or no provocation.

The feud was said to have ended with the Battle of Grapevine Creek when the governor ordered special marshals to end the feud by whatever means necessary. Others would say the feud continued to 1921 when coal mining disputes enraged the two factions once again. "How many lives were taken by the guns of the feudists will never be determined. Some chroniclers have placed the total at twenty-odd; others at fifty or sixty; still others at hundreds."[6]

How ironic that the patriarchs of the two clans were untouched by the gunfire that permeated the lives of the mountain people. Randolph McCoy had been "poisoned" by the feud. "The family war was his most common topic of conversation. He would talk about it at the slightest provocation."[7] At the home of his nephew, the 90-year-old fell into an open fire, was severely burned, and obviously would not survive. "He went to his grave still 'a-cussin' the Hatfields, still thinking of injustices he had never avenged."[8]

In 1910 when two more of Devil Anse's sons were killed, the 72-year-old patriarch came to the realization that nothing could be done to avenge their deaths. At this turning point in Anse's life, a Hardshell Baptist preacher who had fought with Anse in the war, met with his former captain. William Dyke Garrett had often tried to share salvation with the clan leader, but Anse always held him off until this day. "Devil Anse dominated the conversation. He seemed to have something on his mind. Slowly stroking his long beard, he in time turned the talk to religion, and before many minutes had passed, Dyke knew he had added another to his long list of converts."[9] With their leader's conversion, the Hatfields stacked their arms. "Never again in his late years would Devil Anse mention his family troubles. That was a chapter he had locked up the day Dyke Garrett plunged him under the waters of Main Island Creek."[10]

On January 8, 1921, *The New York Times* carried this news item, dated the previous day:

> Anderson Hatfield, long nicknamed "Devil Anse" for his exploits in the Hatfield-McCoy feud that brought violent deaths to so many members of both clans, died quietly in his bed last night of pneumonia at the family home at Island Creek, Logan County. The old mountaineer was in his 86th year. [11]

Hatfield died in good spirits, following weeks of failing health. To the end, he was silent about the feud. "Logan [County] got ready for the biggest funeral in its history."[12]

That kind of constant feuding, bickering, and fussing that characterized the Hatfields and the McCoys even happens in Christianity! The inherent difference, of course, is that we do not settle our feuds with tangible pistols and rifles; our modern-day artillery consists of mouths and minds. The children inherit the fussing of the parents, and the grandchildren inherit the bickering of the parents which causes endless confrontations, endless strife, and an absence of joy. *"There is no peace, saith my God, to the wicked."* (Isaiah 57:21) The one who chooses a wicked course of action will not have peace. The Hatfields and the McCoys had no peace and little, if any, joy. Randolph McCoy went to his grave with no peace. Anderson Hatfield perhaps found peace in the last 11 years of his life. Both men had to live with the heartache and tears of their loved ones.

Joseph knew he had to make a choice. I can almost see the anguish on Joseph's face as he wrestled with the twin nature inside of him. "Do I choose mercy which will bring me joy? Do I choose God?" Romans 8:28, "*...all things work together for good to them that love God, to them who are the called according to his purpose.*" Joseph contemplated, "Do I believe that God had a purpose for my life? Or do I choose vengeance and judgment and the ultimate strife in every resulting evil work?"

Joseph realized that he deserved the same judgment and the same punishment from a just God, and Joseph wisely chose his course of action. He chose mercy—believing that mercy ultimately rules over judgment. Joseph's choice of mercy over judgment brought great joy to his family, to his nation, and to the entire nation of Egypt. When Joseph chose joy, he found joy. The one who chooses mercy will find joy and gladness. Choose wisdom, peace, and mercy because God says, *"Blessed are the merciful: for they shall obtain mercy."* (Matthew 5:7) Suppose Randolph McCoy had chosen mercy over vengeance when he discovered his brother-in-law in possession of one of his hogs? Countless lives would have been untouched by the havoc wreaked over the rightful ownership of one hog.

The Bible says that when Joseph chose mercy, his brothers came before him and bowed. His dream was fulfilled! As they bowed before him, Joseph's emotions burst within him, and he

> "There is no pain so great as the memory of joy in present grief."
> –Aeschylus

had to leave to hide his tears and emotion. At this point in his life, he had a decision to make. With his power from Pharaoh's appointment, he could lord his position over them and make life miserable for his brothers. He could put them in the same prison from which he had been rescued. He could refuse to sell them the only available food to be had because he had the power of Pharaoh behind him, and the whole world wanted Egypt's food. In essence, Joseph was the savior of the world. "What do I do? What do I do?" Joseph agonized.

The second time the brothers came and bowed before him, he asked many questions about his brother Benjamin and his father.

Eventually after testing his brothers, he revealed himself to them. To be sure, great fear fell on Joseph's brothers. I have no doubt they already lived with the constant torment of what they had done to Joseph. Theirs was a great conspiracy, a great secret. As Joseph's brothers matured, I wonder what kind of anguish of soul they had every day of their lives concerning the mistreatment of Joseph.

When Joseph revealed himself as their brother, the Bible says in Genesis 45:3, "...*they were troubled at his presence.*" There was no joy at that moment. I have no doubt the brothers were looking at the whole concept between a man who chose mercy and a group who chose vengeance, and those who had chosen vengeance were now asking for mercy.

Joseph knew that God was bigger than the conspiracy of his brothers! God meant their evil for good, and because of their evil, they were still alive and asking Joseph for provisions. If the brothers had not performed the misdeeds, none of them—not even Joseph—would have been alive. It was good that they thought evil of Joseph. It was good that they sold him into slavery. It was good that they conspired to destroy him. "*And God sent me before you to preserve you a posterity in the earth, and to save your lives by a great deliverance. So now it was not you that sent me hither, but God....*" (Genesis 45:7, 8) When Joseph chose mercy, God catapulted him into the second-in-command position; only Pharaoh ruled above him. Joseph was in the right place, and when he chose mercy and forgiveness, he was given the right position—one that would save the world. Genesis 50:21 says that Joseph nourished them and spoke kindly to them.

To choose mercy over judgment is to choose joy. What does it mean to choose mercy over judgment? To *judge* means "to make decisions of justice" or "fairness" or "to decide what is fair" or "to measure the actions of an individual in the context of justice."

If you were in Joseph's place, how would you judge them? I believe I would be cruel to them and sentence them to death.

They had murdered a young boy in their minds. They sold him and took away his life; yet, my judgment would have been wrong because Joseph, who had the power to judge them severely, chose mercy.

The Meaning of "Mercy Rejoiceth Against Judgment"

1. **A person chooses that which ultimately brings him joy, not sadness.** If Joseph in the final analysis wanted to be a very selfish person, but also wanted to be extremely happy for the rest of his life, he would still choose mercy. Why? Mercy is always the path of joy.

Being selfish and choosing vengeance is a foolish choice to make. Vengeance hurts the person who exercises vengeance. The person who rises up in anger against another who does him wrong is actually hurting himself, bringing greater shame, greater pain, and greater reproach to himself than the person who initially committed the wrong. Yes, he would suffer wrong, but the person choosing vengeance would also suffer wrong. Every time mercy is shown to someone who does not deserve it, the one who shows mercy walks away the happier person.

> "The best manner of avenging ourselves is by not resembling him who has injured us."
> –Jane Porter

Every time someone wrongs you, say, "That is fine. Don't worry about it." Before you rush into a decision of vengeance, look at the anguish on the person's face and hear him saying, "I am so sorry; I can't believe I did that."

You say, "Don't worry about it. You are forgiven. It is all cared for." As you walk away, you can say, "I am happy! I am happy because I showed mercy to someone who knew he did not deserve my mercy."

Criticism, vengeance, and wrath do not bring joy. *"For the wrath of man worketh not the righteousness of God."* (James 1:20)

Lashing out in judgment does not bring right actions and right attitudes. Rather, it ultimately brings strife and bitterness and further judgment. If I ultimately judge another strictly by his misdeeds or strictly by my hurt feelings, then I am telling God, "This is how I want You to judge me."

Believe me, I don't want God to judge me that way! I want God to judge me in mercy.

2. Mercy judges only with the purpose of correcting and helping. Mercy always judges a situation by correcting the problem. Sometimes the motive behind a person's criticism is to invest in another and make him better. Some older and wiser people have earned the right to say, "May I give you a little constructive criticism?"

When people write notes to me that say, "I don't think you should say such-and-such or preach that or teach that or do that or do it that way," I always say, "I'm sure that person is trying to improve me." I have learned the valuable lesson that some of the criticism I receive is actually people trying to invest in me.

I am very slow to react in vengeance because truthfully, I may need the correction and the teaching; I may need to learn. Sometimes people who really want to invest in another person are not tactful and do not always use the right words.

Sometimes your parents spoke harshly to you. They weren't trying to hurt you; they were trying to make you a better person. They may have chosen the wrong method of correction, but their motive was right. A wise young man says, "I think Dad is trying to make a man out of me." Sometimes a mother might take out her frustrations by raising her voice because her daughter won't help her in the kitchen and she spitefully says, "You will be a lousy wife someday." I am reasonably sure she is not trying to hurt her daughter; she is trying to help her. We must understand that sometimes critical words are meant to help us become a better person.

I always receive all criticism with an approachable spirit. I want to be corrected. I never want to say, "I have arrived." I know that the day I believe I have arrived is the day I start accelerating my demise. Ask King Saul about that principle. When Saul was little in his own eyes, God exalted him, but when Saul became king, he began to push down anyone whom he deemed a personal threat. As a result, he forfeited his kingdom. No one can afford to get to the point where he thinks he has arrived. When critics come your way, accept their judgments with a spirit that says, "Maybe I can improve myself."

3. **Mercy judges by fixing a problem.** This point is very similar to the first point, but there is a difference. Let me explain. A plumber "criticizes" by fixing the leak. He doesn't take his wrench, beat the pipes, and call them names. A carpenter doesn't correct or judge by using his hammer to smash a window that did not fit properly.

When the deacons of First Baptist Church met with me to consider purchasing the former NBD bank building on State Street, we judged that building. Every stairwell, every door, every staircase riser, every ceiling, every light fixture, every wall, every floor—every square inch was judged by us. We decided we could make the building usable. We laid new flooring, painted the walls, rewired the electrical system, and installed new lights. We judged the building by fixing it.

The way to criticize is by fixing. For instance, I do not criticize my wife by tearing her down; I criticize (or judge) her by helping her become what she needs to become. I judge my children by giving them the tools they need. I judge my staff by giving them the wherewithal to do their jobs. I judge the church by preaching and helping the people find the will of God for their lives. I do not judge others by tearing them down; I judge others by helping them find the right path. Mercy always judges by fixing.

4. **Mercy judges with the hope of bringing joy to the judged.** If I want to judge my child or one of our school children or a church member or a staff member, my purpose is always to

make those being judged happier. Let me share an illustration. Dr. Wendell Evans, the President of Hyles-Anderson College, used to say, "It is almost worth doing something wrong in order to be reprimanded by Brother Hyles—almost." I have been a recipient of that *almost* situation on more than one occasion. I was judged several times by Brother Hyles, and honestly, every single time was a learning experience for me. I left his presence a better man. I know that today I have more joy than I would have had if I had not been scolded by him. The difference between a scolding by a critic and a scolding by a merciful man is the merciful man says, "I want you to be happy some day."

"We judge ourselves by what we feel capable of doing; others judge us by what we have done."
–Henry Wadsworth Longfellow

The young person who chooses liquor today will not be happy when today's choice escalates into a choice of alcoholism for a lifetime. Just ask the rescue mission men how happy they are because they chose the bottle over family, friends, and respectability. To be sure, they can testify there is no long-term joy in a bottle. There are "...pleasures of sin for a season; but *sin, when it is finished, bringeth forth death.*" (James 1:15b) Not many people are joyful at a funeral—especially when the funeral is for a person who wasted his life. Sin robs you of your joy.

- Mercy judges by saying, "Let's think through this decision carefully."
- Mercy says, "I know you are in love; let's make sure your parents are on the same page."
- Mercy says, "I know you are old enough to get married, but let's make sure we follow the rules."

Ultimately, the person who listens to mercy will look back and say, "I did not know life could be this happy!" There is no joy in divorce or custody battles over children or in paying alimony. There is never any joy in paying the price of a broken relationship. Joy comes to those who do right and accept mercy's judgment.

5. Mercy judges by giving others the benefit of the doubt.
A merciful judge always considers the fact that maybe he is wrong
and the other party might be right. A merciful judge always gives
the other person the benefit of the doubt. He will find more joy in
giving the benefit of the doubt than in saying, "I got my way."

When I was a teenage boy, I learned that when I gave my parents the benefit of the doubt, I walked away the happiest person.
As a college student at Hyles-Anderson, I found when I gave the
administration, the faculty, and the staff the benefit of the doubt,
I was a happier student. As an administrator at Hyles-Anderson
College, I found that if I gave my pastor, who was my employer,
the benefit of the doubt, I ultimately found that I was glad he did
not listen to me and implement some of my ideas.

I said to my wife, "God bless your dad! He listened patiently
to many of my harebrained ideas and schemes." I remember one
in particular when a former faculty member at Hyles-Anderson
College and I had a great idea that to this day is almost too embar-
rassing to admit. Suffice it to say, we were going to win the whole
world to Christ, so we made an appointment with Brother Hyles.
We walked confidently into his office, and he listened and listened
and listened to our plan. Finally, he made one comment, and I
immediately saw his logic and felt the color draining from my face.
I remember thinking, "**Why** are you sitting in here wasting his
time with this really stupid idea? You are 22 years of age, trying to
tell Brother Hyles how to run his ministry when you have never
built anything!"

He finally looked at me and asked, "Was this
your idea?"

I began stuttering.

He was so merciful and gracious. He patted

> "The art of being
> wise is the art of
> knowing what to
> overlook."
> –William James

me on the back and said, "God bless you. Maybe you will grow up
someday. I wasn't very smart when I was your age either." I felt just
tall enough to walk **under** the door as I left his office!

I often think he must be chuckling up in Heaven as he looks

at me over the battlements and says, "Now, you know."

Your parents will keep you from doing something ridiculous; instead of being grateful, you will feel that you were put down. Wait 20 years and you will say, "Was I ever stupid back then!"

When I counsel, I try very hard to resist the urge to say, "Wait until you are my age." Instead, I try to logic with the person, share some common-sense principles, and finally say, "You have not been 45, but I have been 19. You do not know what it is like on this side, but I do know what it is like on that side. Would you please trust me? Then, when you are 45, come and tell me you did the right thing. If I am wrong, I will ask for your forgiveness!" Mercy always says, "I will give you the benefit of the doubt."

6. Mercy judges only within the arena of the merciful. I believe this is the most important point. I would only want to judge someone within the arena of those who can do something about the issue. For instance, if I believe a young person did something wrong at school, it would not be appropriate for me to address the issue in front of the congregation of First Baptist Church. Nor would it be appropriate for me to tell my wife and children about the situation because they cannot fix the problem. That issue needs to be brought to the principals' meeting because that is the arena of the merciful. All of those men on the principals' committee are trying to help every child become the best he can become. In that arena alone, it is acceptable to judge a situation involving a student.

Suppose a husband and a wife seek counsel from me about marriage difficulties. Where is the best place for me to address that situation? Should I call in their children and tell them about their parents' problems? Should they be told all the inside secrets about what is wrong with their parents' marriage? Of course not! The only people who can fix that marriage are the husband and the wife. The three of us work together to that end. Occasionally, I use an illustration from the pulpit, but that is a way of helping to keep other marriages healthy.

I do not take the high school problems to the college. I do not take the college problems to the deacons. I do not take the deacons' problems to the church. I will not take family problems to any audience. I believe in taking problems only to the arena where they can be fixed. Therefore, I find the arena of the merciful—the people who want to help.

Sometimes the only arena I have is Jesus Christ. I take those problems to my prayer closet and say, "God, You alone have the power to correct this situation."

The pastor of a church has a merciful office. Any problem can be addressed in the pastor's office.

How important it is to understand that we judge mercifully by staying within our arena of responsibility!

7. Mercy judges knowing he will be judged by the Judge of the universe. I know that for every judgment I make, I am showing God how I want Him to judge me on every action I make. I believe that every decision I make in a marriage counseling session, about a ministry, about the schools or the college or about how people treat me personally, I am saying, "God, let me show You how I would like You to treat me when You have to judge me." How very important it is to have a lot of mercy when sitting in judgment of anyone!

Often in my counseling I hear a statement like, "But you don't know what someone did to my family!"

"Oh, be careful," I exclaim. "Do you know what **you** did to God?"

"But Brother Schaap," the person retorts, "we are dealing with reality here!"

"Yes! A real God experienced a real cross, shed real blood, suffered real shame, real sin, and a real Hell that you deserve! God showed us at Calvary how He wants us to judge others!"

When Christ was mocked by the jeering crowd standing at the foot of the cross, He said, "Father, forgive them!" Perhaps He felt they did not really know what they were saying. Perhaps some of them wanted to be the center of attention at the moment. Possibly they did not understand that Jesus was dying for their sins. Whatever their reasons for being disrespectful, He wanted God to be easy on them!

Do you copy that kind of forbearance at all when people mistreat you? Do you copy that forgiving spirit when people mistreat your loved ones? Do you copy that kind of love when people mistreat your family? Do you copy that patience when people insult you? Or do you retaliate and say, "I will get even with you if it is the last thing I do!"

If anyone had the right to get even, it was Jesus! He could have found many ways to get even; instead, He said, *"Father, forgive them; for they know not what they do...."* (Luke 23:34)

What else did Jesus do as He faced His tormentors? He asked John to take care of His mother. To a sinner on an adjacent cross, He gave the gift of eternal life in Heaven. Jesus handled His attacks with such an incredible graciousness! He did not get distracted from why He was hanging on the cross; rather, He stayed focused on His purpose and still reacted with great mercy. Why? Mercy brings the greatest joy.

> "God always gives His best to those who leave the choice with Him."
> –Jim Elliot

Christ is our example of how to react when people attack us. Because He reacted with mercy, we can too. If you feel a loved one has been mistreated and in your judgment, someone acted improperly, give them the benefit of the doubt. If you do judge another person, judge with the intent of helping the person, not hurting him. Judge by following the golden rule: Do to them as you would have them do to you. Mercy rejoices in proper judgment and thus brings joy.

*"Let me never be afraid of endings
or beginnings. Teach me to embrace
all of life with joy."*
                                    –Helen Lesman

That Your Joy May Be Full

Suggested Reading:
I John 1:4-10

My premise in chapter one of this book is the very simple fact that to rejoice is a choice. Being a joyful Christian or a dejected, defeated Christian is an individual choice. It seems that too many people are waiting for some joy angel to wave a magic wand or give them a joy pill to make them feel happy. Too many people are waiting for some spiritual lottery, but wishful thinking does not happen spiritually. Joy cannot be chosen randomly. Being full of joy is a choice we make whenever and wherever we choose to be and whenever and wherever we choose to have it.

"In this world, full often, our joys are only the tender shadows which our sorrows cast."
–Henry Ward Beecher

Chapter three addresses the basic ingredients to joy. In the darkest nights and the most wearisome of days I realize my sins are forgiven, Jesus lives, I have an inheritance, I have eternal security in Christ, and I cannot lose my salvation. Nothing can separate me from the love of God! I might experience times of grief or intense sadness, and perhaps times of great shame and reproach, but I can never lose what God has given to me—my eternal life in Christ.

Suppose I am having a very boring day at work or a time of grief. At those times, I can take a personal inventory. When I ask myself, "Are your sins forgiven?" I can say, "Yes, my name is written down in Heaven!" No matter how bad the day gets, I am still going to Heaven. If the day brings an accident or getting fired because of work downsizing or any type of bad news, the bottom line is I am still saved! No matter what kind of world problems threaten, the Christian can be joyful because he knows his Redeemer lives. A Christian may lose his job, but he still has an inheritance in Heaven. That inheritance can never be taken away; after all, God is not an Indian giver! However, taking inventory of these basic ingredients does not determine the intensity of an individual's joy.

In his quest for joy, the Christian encounters two great problems:

1. How can I sustain my joy?
2. How can I deepen the intensity of my joy?

Once I began the journey of joy, I then want to have greater joy. I am also interested in how I can sustain my joy. How can I have it every day?

I remember my predecessor, Brother Hyles, teaching us to figure out the formula when we had a good day. He said to write down those ingredients, commit them to memory, and choose to have a good day anytime by including one or more of those ingredients.

Unfortunately, we Christians sometimes become confused by the difference between joy and happiness. Quite simply, joy is inside, and happiness is outside. Joy is gladness that comes from within. Happiness is gladness that comes to an individual. Too many people confuse joy and happiness. What they called "joy" was actually a pay raise or a Christmas bonus or a nice compliment from the boss or a letter of congratulations or a bill that was reduced or the IRS canceled its tax audit. Any or all of these external catalysts might well cause the Christian to sing, "I have the joy, joy, joy, joy, down in my heart." No, you have the "happiness, happiness, happiness" from a government agency. You have the "happiness, happiness, happiness" from an external employer. You have the "happiness, happiness, happiness," because your wife smiled at you. All this external is happiness—not joy.

Suppose the doctor calls and says you have a life-threatening disease. This particular scenario is one with which I deal almost weekly at First Baptist Church. The person often comes to my office seeking prayer and to be anointed with oil. I met with one good man who said, "Brother Schaap, how do I live with this fatal disease?"

> "Heavy thoughts bring on physical maladies."
> –Martin Luther

"My brother," I said, "You might die from walking out of this building and getting hit by a car or a bus. This disease might not kill you. Put a happy look on your face and enjoy what you have!" Not long after that appointment, he wrote me a letter and shared that a doctor's report came back and magically the disease was gone! What wonderful news! This church member has both joy and happiness. He has happiness from the doctor's unexpected good report and has joy because he knows God did something special for him.

Much of what we call joy is simply the external—good things happening to us in our life. Sustaining happiness means the external has to keep working all the time. For instance, the boss has to be kept happy or he will find reason to see that his employee has an unhappy day. If our happiness is what we are trying to sustain, we have to have many external happenings. We have to regularly go to a theme park or amusement parks like Great America. We have to have a regular pay raise. We have to regularly receive work promotions. We have to have regular compliments from the boss. Our family members have to be healthy and strong and positive; otherwise, we lose our happiness.

However, the Christian cannot worry so much about his personal happiness; what he needs to address is his inner joy. That inside joy is maintained by God. Not only can He sustain it, He can deepen it and give the Christian greater joy. I John 1:4 says, "...*that your joy may be full*." Every Christian needs the full joy that God says he can have. *Full joy* means "sustained joy." We can have the same joy tomorrow that we had today as well as every day thereafter. *Full joy* also means "more joy"; the literal Greek word means "to cram it full until it is overflowing."

"Joys divided are increased."
–J. G. Holland

We can actually have joy that spills over so other people know that we are joyful. That joy can be sustained day after day after day. When the Welshman, Billy Bray, got saved, he had been a wicked, drunken, filthy-mouthed miner. He gave up smoking and drinking forever. Though his friends thought he would soon return to his former worldly ways, he never did! It is said that he never met a person without inquiring as to the condition of his soul. His life was almost immediately characterized by the joy of the Lord, and his was a shouting religion. Billy Bray testified that when he got saved, he felt the joy bells ringing in his head. "I can't help praising God," he would say, "As I go along the street I lift up one foot, and it seems to say 'Glory!' and I lift up the other, and it seems to say, 'Amen!'; and so they keep on like that all the time I am walking."[1] Characterized by a radiant joy, he became a fervent soul winner. He was sometimes criticized for his intensity, but his love for God was very real.

When his wife died, Billy jumped about the room with ecstasy, exclaiming, "Bless the Lord! My dear Joey is gone up with the shining angels! Glory! Glory! Glory!" The goodness of God made him glad even in times of sorrow. On his deathbed he asked the doctor who told him he was dying, "When I get up there, shall I give them your compliments, doctor, and tell them you will be coming too?" The doctor was tremendously touched. Bray continued, "What? Me fear death! Me lost? Why, my Saviour conquered death. If I were to go down to Hell I would shout, 'Glory! glory! Unto my blessed Jesus until I made the bottomless pit ring again,' and that miserable ol' Satan would say, 'Billy, Billy, this is no place for thee; get thee back.' Then up to Heaven I would go, shouting, 'Glory, glory, praise the Lord!' "[2]

Bray died of consumption at 74 years of age still praising the Lord.

The story is told that some of the miners who heard him preach accused him of being crazy. Billy Bray just replied, "Yes, I am *crazy* about Jesus, Who is crazy about me! I am just so full that God would be so good to a wicked, foul-mouthed sinner like me! I just never will get over that!"

Some people never do get over their salvation. Their joy bubbles up like a well overflowing. Seemingly, every movement these joy-filled Christians make in life is filled with an eternal joy. The goodness of God never leaves them!

A Christian can have joy every day, and he can have more intense joy if he so desires. The Apostle John, who wrote the three little books—I John, II John, and III John—tells us how to sustain our joy and how to deepen our joy if we want to know.

Pain, sorrow, disappointment, could not beat down his ardor. Whether he [Billy Bray] was gathering miners to pray in the depths underground, or faced some winter tempest in a soul-winning expedition to some distant village, or whether he was shouting in the pulpit of a tiny chapel, he was faithful unto the end with his, "Bless the Lord, bless the Lord. If they were to put me into a barrel, I would shout 'Glory!' through the bunghole!" Lord!' "[3]

1. Having sustained joy is directly related to a Christian's relationship with sin. He must be sure that nothing sinful robs him of his fellowship with God. *"If we say that we have fellowship with him, and walk in darkness, we lie, and do not the truth."* (I John 1:6) Having fellowship with Him **and** walking in darkness is impossible.

If you say that you have fellowship with God but don't, He says you will never know what real sustained, deep joy is. You are relying only upon happiness—the external things that give you what you call joy. You will never have a day-by-day intense joy.

2. The degree of a Christian's joy is related to his fellow-

ship with God. He must understand who his Partner is. The Christian who doesn't choose the right partner in life will not have sustained joy. Just saying or just pretending that God is your partner does not make it so. Certainly I can say I am in business with Ford Motor Company, but I doubt that I will be a recognized shareholder or receive a salary. Just making a statement does not make it so. John says to make sure you are in partnership with God.

My father-in-law, Brother Hyles, had the most sustained joy and the deepest joy of any person I ever knew. He had discovered a fountain of joy because he walked with God.

The advice he always gave to every preacher boy at Hyles-Anderson College was to walk with God. No one walked with God with as much intensity as my father-in-law, the former pastor of First Baptist Church of Hammond, Indiana. We never failed to laugh during his sermons, even when we were being scolded. He was a man of joy, and I cannot help but think of him often because he possessed what I wanted—sustained, deep, intense joy. How intense my joy is, is determined by my relationship with God. What exactly is fellowship?

• **Partnership.** When I was growing up, I found that certain things brought me joy, but I did not know why they brought me joy. Possibly I heard someone preach about it, or as I have studied the Bible through the years, I learned to apply the principle in my Christian life. For as far back as I can remember, I have always used the word "partner" when I talked to God. I have always found incredible satisfaction in the thought of having a partnership relationship with God.

Who is my partner in life? As far as an earthly partner of life, my wife is my partner. We talk together and walk through life together. When I think about my ministry or my profession, I always say, "God, You and I are partners in life." I want to walk with God and talk to God just like I walk and talk with my earthly partner.

My introduction to a partnership goes back to the days when I was an 11-year-old boy, and my dad brought me into his employ. As we worked together year after year, we grew closer and closer. I enjoyed hearing Dad say to me, "Son, you are my partner. Someday, I will make you my official partner. Someday this business will be yours." I greatly enjoyed that partnership relationship with my father very much. However, when I got called to preach, I realized that my dad and I were going in different directions. I realized that my Heavenly Father and I were going to be partners, and that relationship is available to every born-again believer!

> "How many hopes and fears, how many ardent wishes and anxious apprehensions are twisted together in the threads that connect the parent with the child!"
> –Samuel Griswold Goodrich

However, many Christians go for days without thinking about Who He is. How can we possibly have a partnership with a person we do not even acknowledge? The only time some people are vaguely aware of Him is when they come to church and are reminded of Him.

Years ago when I was a young college freshman at a college in Minnesota, a guest preacher shared an illustration about Charles Haddon Spurgeon, the great Baptist preacher of London, England. Charles Spurgeon said, "I have never gone for more than 15 minutes in my life without being consciously aware that God is with me."

The story is oft repeated how Spurgeon and two friends were crossing a busy London street with many carriages and horses passing to and fro. Just as Spurgeon stepped off the curb and took a few steps into the street, he felt a cloud of doubt pass between him and God. He stopped immediately and bowed his head. His partners dodged the horses and carriages and made it safely to the other side of the street. They turned to see Mr. Spurgeon standing in the street with his head bowed in prayer.

"God, there is a cloud of doubt between You and me,"

"He taught his people to pray, doing so far more by his example than by any preaching. People heard him pray with such reality that they became ashamed of their own mere repetition of words."[5]

Spurgeon prayed, "and I don't want to get to the other side of the street before I take care of that cloud of doubt." When Spurgeon felt his relationship with God was right, he continued to the other side of the street.

D. L. Moody, after his first visit to England, being asked upon his return to America, "Did you hear Spurgeon preach?" He replied, "Yes, but better still I heard him pray."[4]

When I heard that preacher's illustration, my heart was greatly stirred. I said, "Lord, can that be possible? Can that be real? Can I wake up in the middle of the night and be aware of You? Can I awaken in the morning and be aware of You? Can I go to bed at night and say, 'God, good day or bad day, it was You and me all day long today' "? That kind of relationship and partnership is what I desired in my life. I realized that partnering with God meant spending time with God.

Many a Christian's joy is missing because he partners with the world and what the world offers. He partners with the music that is not of God. He partners with the language that is not of God. He partners with the darkness that does not belong to God.

God asks, "How can you say you have fellowship with Me when you partner with my enemies?" "*If we say that we have fellowship with him, and walk in darkness, we lie, and do not the truth.*" (I John 1:6) The person who partners with the world will not have sustained joy! A Christian's degree of joy is related to his fellowship—his partnership—with God. Fellowship has a second meaning.

• **Participation.** Enjoying with God the things which God enjoys is participation. For example, if my wife and I decide to go out to eat, I know her favorite restaurant is Teibel's, and her favorite meal is perch. One Friday morning I said to her, "Let's go out to eat tonight. I will meet you at 5:30 at Teibel's."

After we were both seated, the waitress came to take the

order, and I said, "She would like the fish." I could confidently order for my wife because I know what she likes, and we participate together. I didn't take her to Arby's because she doesn't like Arby's. I participate in things she likes, and that participation brings me joy.

Some Christians spend their whole life trying to figuratively twist God's arm to see it their way. Their whole preoccupation spiritually is:

"May I please marry the person of whom nobody approves?"

"May I please go to a college of which nobody approves?"

"May I please live a life that is unpleasing to my parents, my pastor, and to You God, but please bless me while I am doing it."

"May I please spend my money on the things I want—not tithe and give offerings?"

"May I please live where I want to live and do what I want to do?"

"God, can I divorce the one to whom I am married and get somebody else to make me happy?"

"By the way, God, what is Your problem? Why can't You make me happy?"

These kinds of questions remind me of a young married man who made an appointment to see me when I was working at Hyles-Anderson College. He said, "Brother Schaap, I have prayed about this matter, and I know already what you are going to tell me, but God has given me peace about it. I know it is the will of God that I divorce my wife and marry my sweetheart."

I merely asked, "What do you want me to say?"

"I want your blessing," he stated.

"You are a moron," I said. "I will not tell you that your plan is acceptable. I love you, but you are a spiritual idiot." Too many Christians live their lives in such a ludicrous, cockamamie way. We are like what I call Burger King Christians as we say to God, "I want the joy, joy, joy, joy down in my heart, but I want it **my** way!" We want to order our lives our way, live the way we want to live, and then we want God's blessing—His stamp of approval. We cannot understand why we are not happy!

The answer is very simple! You have not fellowshipped with God. You have not partnered with Him, and you have not participated in that which makes Him happy.

What is participation? For many years my grandfather owned a trailer park in Holland, Michigan. Once a month my grandfather had to take the trash to the dump. One day he said to me, "I'd like you to go to the dump with me."

"I don't want to go to the dump," I emphatically stated.

"Why not?" Grandpa wanted to know.

"Because it stinks there!"

So I did not go with Grandpa. About three hours later, I saw one of my friends enjoying what was left of an ice cream cone. "Where did you get that?" I asked him.

"I went with your grandpa to the dump," he said. "We stopped at the ice cream shop on the way home."

I immediately went to see my grandpa. "You didn't tell me you were going to the ice cream store, Grandpa," I accused.

"I wasn't planning on going to the ice cream store," he explained. "I was going to the dump."

Realizing that I had missed out on a treat, I hurriedly said, "Can I go with you?"

"I am not going for another whole month."

Believe me, the next month I spent Friday night at Grandpa's house so I could get up early Saturday morning and help Grandpa go to the dump. Bright and early, I ran into his bedroom, jumped on his belly, and said, "Grandpa! Grandpa! Grandpa! Time for the dump!"

He looked at his watch and said, "It is only six o'clock in the morning, son! Go back to bed!"

"But Grandpa," I coaxed, "we need to go to the dump!"

"Why are you so anxious to go? A month ago, you didn't want to go to the dump," Grandpa questioned.

"I love going to the dump," I said. "Besides, I am a whole month older now! I am a big boy."

I finally talked Grandpa into leaving early. We loaded up the trailer and went to the dump! It was just like I remembered—stinky and smelly. But on the way home, we stopped at Mill's Ice Cream Parlor, and I ordered a triple-dip butter pecan ice cream cone! My participation with Grandpa earned me a triple-dip ice cream cone! By the way, I never again missed going with Grandpa to the dump!

> "Try not to become a man of success, but rather try to become a man of value."
> –Albert Einstein

One day I was doing some minor house repair, and I needed some supplies from the hardware store. I said to my daughter Jaclynn, "I have to go to Schillings. Want to go with me?"

"Do they have any food there?"

"No, there is no food at Schilling Lumber."

"Then I am not going to go," she said.

"You are going to be sorry," I warned.

"I still do not want to go," she decided.

So I went to Schilling Brothers Lumber and picked up all the supplies I needed. On the way home I noticed that the Dairy Queen marquee sign was advertising peanut buster parfaits for $.99, so I stopped and bought one. As I drove into the driveway at home, I was enjoying the last of my treat. I walked inside the house carrying my bag of supplies and the container for the peanut buster parfait.

Jaclynn saw me and the container at the same time. "Dad," she pointed, "what is that?"

"It was a delicious peanut buster parfait."

"Did you get that at Schilling Brothers Lumber?"

"No, I got it at Dairy Queen."

"Dad," she charged, "you didn't tell me you were going to Dairy Queen."

"I wasn't going to Dairy Queen," I explained. "I went to the hardware store."

"Dad, if I had gone with you, could I have gone to Dairy Queen?"

"Probably," I stated matter-of-factly.

"But Dad, why didn't you tell me?"

"Because Jaclynn, I didn't plan on going there."

Jaclynn learned if she had participated with me, she would have received the benefits of going with me. That example illustrates perfectly what joy is; it is participating with God.

Fellowship with God is participating with the things God would do if He were on earth today. The conversation might be as follows: "God, where are You going today?"

"I am going to go win some people to Me. I am going to share the Gospel. I am going to go to a prison and preach."

"But God, all that sounds so boring. Where else are You going to go?

"I am going to go to a nursing home and bring forgotten people on buses to church. I am also going to get up at 2:30 a.m., get on a bus, go to Chicago, find some of the homeless people, put them on buses, and bring them to church."

To some Christians, seeking and saving the lost does not sound like much fun. How is your joy level? The reason you have no joy is because you have no desire to partnership or participate with God. If you are going to fellowship with God, you must be His partner!

Not only does fellowship with God mean partnering with God and participating with God, it has yet another meaning.

• **Communion with God.** Your level of joy is directly measured by your communion with God.

> "Ere you left your room this morning,
> Did you think to pray?
> In the name of Christ our Saviour,
> Did you sue for loving favor,
> As a shield today?"

Every morning my wife and I get up early to spend time in the Word of God and to commune with God.

> "Sweet hour of prayer! Sweet hour of prayer!
> That calls me from a world of care,
> And bids me at my Father's throne,
> Make all my wants and wishes know."

Too many Christians go to God only during a foxhole crisis. God should not be treated like a 911 button. Rather, Christians must maintain a daily walk with God because joy comes from fellowshipping with God.

Joy is an inner strength, an inner calm that peacefully meets every circumstance in life—both the negative and the positive. *"He that dwelleth in the secret place of the most High shall abide under the shadow of the Almighty. I will say of the LORD, He is my refuge and my fortress: my God; in him will I trust."* (Psalm 91:1, 2) Instead of communing with God Who is a strong tower, some people partner and commune with sin and iniquity, and they wonder why they have no lasting joy! When was the last time you did commune with Him?

A question I hear so often is, "How long should I pray Brother Schaap?"

I always answer, "Pray till your heart gets tender. Pray until you realize how good God is."

Another question I hear equally as often is, "How long should I read my Bible?"

Basically, I give the same answer: "Read until your heart burns!"

"Prayer is the key of the morning and the bolt of the evening."
–Mahatma Gandhi

I often find myself reading and reading and needing to stop because of my schedule, but wanting to read more. When you almost cannot force yourself to stop reading the Bible, you know you have read long enough! Your heart will soar with joy after communing with Him in His book. You sustain

"Reading is to the mind what exercise is to the body."
–Joseph Addison

your joy and deepen your joy by communing with Him.

Christian, you will have joy to the degree you have fellowship with God. Having fellowship with God means partnering with Him, participating with Him, and communing with Him.

*"God didn't promise days without pain,
laughter without sorrow, sun without rain,
but He did promise strength for the day,
comfort for the tears, and light for the way."*
    –Author Unknown

How to Sustain My Joy

Suggested Reading:
I John 1:4-10

In the previous chapter, I used I John 1:4-10 to teach the principle of how to deepen your joy. We established that deeper joy comes from fellowship with God. Having fellowship with God means to be partners with God and to participate with Him in the things that God wants to do. Fellowship with God means to commune with God and to draw closer to Him.

Not only should the Christian want to deepen his joy; he should also want to sustain his joy. Every once in a while, every Christian stumbles over an occasional happy day, but most of them do not know how to relive that day. Also much of what we call joy is actually happiness which is the direct result of something good happening to us.

"Sadness flies on the wings of the morning and out of the heart of darkness comes the light."
    –Jean Giraudoux

As a matter of fact, the words *happening* and *happiness* are derived from "a happening." When that something good happens to us, we say we found joy, but joy is not found in external happenings. Don't get me wrong—there is nothing wrong with good things happening. I like them to happen to me as well as to the next person, but the source of my joy should not be dependent

"If we cannot live so as to be happy, let us at least live so as to deserve it."

–I. H. Fichte

upon what is happening around me. For then, if bad things happen, the person must lose his joy. If bad things continually happen, the person becomes depressed.

However, if we understand that joy comes from within, as the Bible teaches, then we can decide to have joy anytime we desire to have joy! Since many Christians do not know how to find the joy within them because of ignorance, they revert back to waiting for something external to motivate the internal to bring us happiness.

Sometimes an external source such as music can motivate an internal source that brings joy. At the very simplest form then, a Christian should be able to control some external stimuli. For instance, if I know that "Blessed Assurance" brings me an inward feeling of joy, then every time I listen to the song, "Blessed Assurance," I can better control the joy within me. Perhaps I know that listening to a favorite sermon will bring me some internal joy; every time I want joy, I can listen to a good sermon.

As I have already stated, we get deeper joy by entering into fellowship—participation, partnership, and communion—with God. Now, that we have established ways to have joy, I want to address the matter of how to sustain that joy. What happens to most Christians is that we have peaks of joy—great feelings within that last for a markedly brief time. We hear Zion's songs, and joy soars within our hearts for the length of the song. Sustained joy is not a euphoric, external happiness, but a calm inner peace and joy.

The Bible says in I John 1:5, "…*that God is light, and in him is no darkness at all.*" He is the only true source of light there is. As we get away from the light, many shadows and darkness envelop us. I John 1:7 says, "*But if we walk in the light, as he is in the light, we have **fellowship** one with another….*" The key word is fellowship, and the fellowship we enjoy with God causes us to have joy.

Obviously the closer we get to the light, the more joy we will find. The more distance the Christian puts between himself and the light the less joy he has. Therefore, a Christian's joy is entirely related to how close he is to the source of light, and his lack of joy is directly related to how distant he is from that light. The Christian who wants to sustain his joy simply stays in the light. If he stays in the light, then he has joy. If he stays and stays and stays and stays and stays in the light, he has and he has and he has and he has joy! However, if he decides to step away from the light, immediately darkness envelopes him, and he loses his joy.

How to Sustain Joy

Please take careful note of the following points which will help every Christian sustain his joy:

1. **Reside in the kingdom of light.** There are two kingdoms. One is the kingdom of darkness, and one is a kingdom of light. Since the Bible says that *"God is light,"* the kingdom of light is God's kingdom. The kingdom of darkness is Satan's kingdom. The Christian who wants to have joy must ally himself with God's kingdom, which is the kingdom of light. Quite simply, if he does not want to have joy, he resides in the kingdom of darkness which is Satan's kingdom.

2. **God is the kingdom of light; His king-dom is light.**

3. **There is a kingdom of darkness.** When we say "darkness," we are addressing ignorance, confusion, unbelief, deception, hypocrisy, lies, and false religion. One of the great reasons why

> "Those who bring sunshine to the lives of others cannot keep it from themselves."
> – J. M. Barrie

Christians lack joy in their lives is because they have bought into the lies of Satan. They have bought into the kingdom of darkness even though they call themselves the children of light.

Let me explain. The Bible says if I am a saved man, I am a child of light. Logic says if I am a child of light, I should not be walking in ignorance. I should leave my false church and get into a true church. If I am a child of light, then I should stop believing the old kingdom of darkness. That in which I was trusting to go to Heaven is no longer the correct answer! Therefore, I must logically find a church that preaches light with the "light" Bible and the "light" truth.

Light is the opposite of darkness. If darkness is deception, then light is truth and sincerity. If darkness is ignorance, then light is truth. If darkness is confusion, then light is understanding. So darkness is confusion, deception, hypocrisy, and lies; on the other hand, light is truth, reality, sincerity, and all that God is. Light is love which means darkness must be hatred.

The suicide bombings so prevalent in several nations is not indicative of a kingdom of light; rather, they depict the kingdom of darkness. It does not matter what religious label is affixed to a suicide bombing; when human beings are slaughtered and injured in the name of God, the people who perpetrate such shockingly brutal acts are not in the kingdom of light! The anger, hostility, and vengeance being committed in such a heinous way is directly related to a kingdom of darkness. No joy exists in the suicide bomber, and certainly no joy comes to the families of those he slaughtered in the name of his false god. A kingdom of light should bring joy, gladness, and peace to people; not ignorance, confusion, unbelief, deception, hypocrisy, and death.

4. I am a child of light. When I trusted Christ as my Saviour, I was born again! I became a child of light, and I also received the light into me. Jesus said, *"...I am the light of the world: he that followeth me shall not walk in darkness...."* (John 8:12)

Many religions embrace different ideology about how to go to Heaven. Jesus said in John 14:6, *"...I am the way, the truth, and the life: no man cometh unto the Father, but by me."* If every religion says theirs is the right way, then someone is lying! Jesus Christ cannot be the liar because He is the truth! Darkness spawns ignorance, hostility, and no joy because people refuse to walk in the light.

When I trusted Christ as my Saviour, *"the light of the world"* came to live within me and even now resides within me—

"...*Christ in you, the hope of glory.*" (Colossians 1:27) I allow that light to expose and do its work, and it exposes the darkness that is in me and around me. If I refuse to confess the darkness that is exposed by the light, I am thereby refusing a deeper fellowship with God. If I choose to refuse a deeper fellowship with God, I am also refusing the deeper joy that the light can give me.

Why are so many Christians unhappy? Why can children of God, who claim the name of Jesus Christ as their Saviour, who have the Light of the world residing inside of them, have such an absence of joy—such a continual, habitual lack of happiness? Some scientists say during certain months of the year that people suffer more with depression because of the lack of light.

In fact, "records exist from 1845 of patients with symptoms that we now know to be indications of SAD (seasonal affective disorder), with accompanying doctors' recommendations that the patients winter in sunny Italy instead of Belgium. Later in the nineteenth century, a ship's doctor observed that his crew was becoming increasingly lethargic during the dark days of an Arctic winter; he recommended that their languor be treated with light.[1]

SAD is very treatable. Sunlight and good-quality indoor lighting are part of a healthy lifestyle. Lack of light is the key factor in SAD.

At the beginning of the twentieth century, more than 70 percent of Americans worked outside. Today, an estimated thirty-eight million North Americans suffer the effects of malillumination (inadequate lighting). Poor lighting creates poor work conditions, which can result in decreased energy and productiveness.[2]

Quite simply, take advantage of sunlight and get outside for at least 20 minutes a day. "Exercise treats both body and mind and is well known for its success in alleviating many forms of depression."[3] The best kind of exercise is what you enjoy the most.

I agree that we do need sunlight for wellness, but often depression is not the result of the lack of sunlight; it is the lack of the Light of the world. We born-again children of God refuse to let the Light do its work. The Light exposes the fact that I have darkness inside of me. The Light exposes my ignorance, my hypocrisy, my lying, my deceit, and my insincerity.

When I see the darkness the Light has exposed, I have a choice to make. Do I acknowledge that darkness, confess my sins, and acknowledge the fact that as I walk closer to Him, I am exposed a little more to the darkness within me? Or do I purposely ignore my conceit, my pride, my arrogance, my hypocrisy, my anger, my wrath toward others, my deceitfulness, my insincerity, my sins, my injustices, and the wicked, hypocritical way I treat others which are all draped and hidden by my ignorance when the Light exposes that I have a decision to make? Do I say to God, "You are right, and I am wrong"? Do I confess my sins?

As I have gotten closer to the Light and the Light has exposed the darkness within me, the two natures have begun to battle. One says, "I don't see what is dark about me!"

The other says, " 'If we say that we have not sinned, we make him a liar....' God, I confess, Your light is right, and I am a sinner."

Confession allows the Christian to walk deeper into the Light. As he walks deeper into the Light, his joy increases. As he walks more deeply into the Light, more darkness is exposed. As he becomes more aware of more darkness, he says, "God I walked more deeply in the Light, and I am more aware of the darkness within me. I acknowledge it, and I confess it. I am wrong, and You are right."

God tells the Christian to move more deeply in the Light. Each time the Christian allows the Light to expose his darkness, and each time he confesses that darkness, he sustains his joy. The moment he says, "I don't see any darkness," he drifts into the shadows and loses his joy. If he refuses to confess the darkness exposed, he is refusing deeper fellowship with God. If he does not want to walk toward the Light, he is saying, "God, I don't want to make You a partner with me. I don't want to participate in the things that please You, and I do not want to commune with You."

The man who refuses to partner with God will be partners with the world. James 4:4 says, *"...know ye not that the friendship of the world is enmity with God? whosoever therefore will be a friend of the world is the enemy of God."* The world is filled with darkness because men love darkness rather than light. Why? Because his deeds are evil. *"And this is the condemnation, that light is come into the world, and men loved darkness rather than light, because their deeds were evil."* (John 3:19) However, the closer the Christian gets to the Source of the light, the more aware he becomes of his failure and how good God is. The purpose of the light isn't just to expose the darkness in me; it is to find out just how faithful God is! *"If we confess our sins, he is faithful and just to forgive us our sins, and to cleanse us from all unrighteousness."* (I John 1:9) God is faithful whether or not a Christian confesses his sin. Then why must a Christian confess his sin? He sustains his joy by confessing his sin!

The Bible says in I John 1:9 that if I confess my darkness (my sins), God is faithful and just to forgive my sins. The word *confession* has several meanings:

- "To agree with." I agree with God and say, "God, there is darkness in me."
- "To covenant." Confession says, "God, I would like to covenant with You. I would like to enter into a special unique relationship with You to seek the Light." The person who covenants with God is willing to see it like God sees it. When he confesses, he becomes enlightened and more aware of truth.

Instead of covenanting with God and seeking the light, sup-

> "The man who refuses to partner with God will be partners with the world."

pose a person chooses darkness. His refusing to acknowledge the light does not remove the light. The light is still shining! No matter how a Christian chooses to live, he cannot shut off the light! The light of the world is Jesus Christ! That Light is faithful! When the person chose darkness, God still sent His blessings—the warmth of the sun, the summer rain, the love and affection of family.

When a Christian covenants with God his life is blessed as he learns the truths of God. "Great is thy faithfulness, O God my Father." God is faithful, just, and fair. As the Christian walks in the light, he becomes more aware of what God has always been. That knowledge brings joy.

> "Just a closer walk with Thee,
> Grant it, Jesus, is my plea;
> Daily walking close to Thee,
> Let it be, dear Lord, let it be."

As we walk closer to God, we see the wonderful truth that He is always faithful to us even when we are unfaithful to Him. As we draw close to that Light, we will discover not that He suddenly becomes faithful; He is always faithful to us!

> "In my moments of peace, through every pain, every tear,
> There's a God who's been faithful to me.
> When my strength is all gone, when my heart had no song,
> Still in love He proved faithful to me.
> Every word He promised is true.
> What I thought was impossible, I see my God do!
>
> He's been faithful, faithful to me.
> Looking back, His love and mercy I see.
> Though in my heart I have questions, even fail to believe,
> Yet He's been faithful, faithful to me.
>
> When my heart looked away, the many times I could not pray,

Still my God, He was faithful to me.
The days I spent so selfishly, reaching out for what pleased
    me,
Even then, God was faithful to me!
Every time I come back to Him,
He is waiting with open arms, and I see once again!

He's been faithful, faithful to me.
Looking back, His love and mercy I see.
Though in my heart I have questions, even fail to believe,
Yet He's been faithful, faithful to me."

The person who lives in that realm of understanding His faithfulness knows that no matter what sins or trespasses he has committed

"One joy dispels a hundred cares."
– Confucius

against God or man, God is constantly faithful to him. That degree of faithfulness brings the fullness of joy in his own soul. It does not matter what is happening externally. The murmurings and threatenings of war in the world do not bring joy, but neither should it remove joy. The joy comes because we know we have a God Who is faithful to us—even when we fail Him. Our joy is found in the fact that we have a God Who never lets us down. Step in the light, for that is where the joy is found!

*"The most profound joy has more
of gravity than of gaiety in it."*
        –Michel de Montaigne

Endnotes

Introduction
[1]"Seize the day!"

[2]Dennis C. Daley, Ph.D. and Howard B. Moss, M.D., *Dual Disorders* (Center City, Minn.: Hazelden, 2002), 161.

[3]American Psychiatric Association, *Diagnostic and Statistical Manual of Mental Disorders, Fourth Edition, Text Revision* (Washington, DC: American Psychiatric Association, 2000), 356.

[4]*DSM-IV-TR*, xxxvii.

[5]Ian H. Gotlib and Susan A. Nolan, contributing editors, "Depressive Disorders," *Psychopathology in Adulthood*, Second Edition (Boston: Allyn & Bacon, 2000), 163.

[6]Linda Wasmer Smith, *Depression: What It Is, How to Beat It* (Berkeley Heights, N.J.: Enslow Publishers, Inc., 2000), 12.

[7]Keith Kramlinger, M.D., Editor in Chief, *Mayo Clinic on Depression* (Rochester, Minn.: Mayo Clinic Health Information, 2001), iii.

[8]John Medina, Ph.D, *Depression: How It Happens, How It Heals* (n.c.: CME, Inc. and New Harbinger Publications, Inc., 1998), 120.

[9]Dr. John Preston, *You Can Beat Depression: A Guide to Prevention and Recovery*, Third Edition (Atascadero, Calif.: Impact Publishers, Inc, 2001), 117-18.

[10]Harold H. Bloomfield, M.D. and Peter McWilliams, *How to Heal Depression* (Los Angeles: Prelude Press, 1994), 110.

Chapter One

[1]Cover Story, "Young and Depressed," *Newsweek*, Volume CXL, No. 15, 7 Oct. 2002, 3.

[2]Pat Winget and Barbara Kantrowitz, "Young and Depressed," *Newsweek*, Volume CXL, No. 15, 7 Oct. 2002, 55.

[3]*Ibid.*, 56.

[4]*Ibid.*, 57.

[5]*Ibid.*, 59-60.

[6]Ian H. Gotlib and Susan A. Nolan, contributing editors, "Depressive Disorders," *Psychopathology in Adulthood*, Second Edition (Boston: Allyn & Bacon, 2000) p. 252.

[7]Winget and Kantrowitz, 60.

[8]*Ibid.*

[9]*Ibid.*

[10]Michael D. Lemonick, "The Mood Molecule," *Time*, Vol. 150, No. 13, 29 September 1997, 76.

[11]Medina, 94.

[12]*"Take heed…"* Exodus 10:28; 19:12; 34:12; Deuteronomy 2:4; 4:9; 4:15; 4:23; 11:16; 12:13; 12:19; 12:30; 27:9; Joshua 22:5; 23:11; I Samuel 19:2; I Kings 2:4; 8:25; I Chronicles 22:13; 28:10; II Chronicles 6:16; 19:6, 7; Ezra 4:22; Job 36:21; Psalm 119:9; Isaiah 7:4; 21:7; Jeremiah 9:4; 17:21; Hosea 4:10; Malachi 2:15, 16; Matthew 6:1; 16:6; 18:10; 24:4; Mark 13:9; Luke 8:18; 12:15; 17:3; 21:8; 21:34; Acts 5:35; 20:28; I Timothy 4:16

[13]Lemonick, 76-77.

[14]Kramlinger, 4.

[15]Margaret Moser and Bill Crawford, *Rock Stars Do the Dumbest Things* (New York: St. Martin's Books, 1998), 43.

[16]American Psychiatric Association, 92.

[17]Sahley, Billie Jay, Ph.D., *The Natural Way to Control Hyperactivity*, San Antonio: Pain & Stress Therapy Center Publications, 1994.

[18]Josephine Wright, M.D., *Do We Really Need Ritalin? A Family Guide to Attention Deficit Hyperactivity Disorder* (New York: Avon Books, 1997), 86.

[19] Doris Rapp, M.D., *Is This Your Child's World?* (New York: William Morrow & Co., 1991), 12.

[20] Wright, 97-98.

[21] Lilly to Add Warning to Strattera Label, Indianapolis, September 29, 2005, http://www.cbsnews.com/stories/2005/09/20/ap/business/main.

[19] Bloomfield, 112.

Chapter Four

[1] Seer Cancer Statistic Review, 1975-2002: Lifetime Risk (Percent) of Being Diagnosed With Cancer, http://seer.cancer.gov/SR/1975_2002/results_single/sect_01_table.14.

Chapter Five

[1] Stephen Braun, *The Science of Happiness: Unlocking the Mysteries of Mood* (New York: John Wiley & Sons, Inc., 2000), 9.

Chapter Six

[1] Don Nardo, *The Battle of Marathon* (San Diego: Lucent Books, 1996), 55.

[2] *Ibid.*, 64.

[3] *Ibid.*, 64.

[4] Paul Ostapuk, "The First Marathon Run: The History of Phidippides," http://www.lakepowell.net/marathon.html, 11/29/2005, 2.

[5] According to the Gale Encyclopedia of Medicine, hyponatremia is defined as a condition that occurs when the sodium in the blood plasma falls below 130 mm. The normal concentration of sodium in the blood plasma is 136-145 mm. Plasma sodium levels of 125 mm or less are dangerous and can result in seizures and coma. Marathon running, under certain conditions, leads to

hyponatremia. Races of 25-50 miles can result in the loss of great quantities (8 to 10 liters) of sweat, which contains both sodium and water. Studies show that about 30% of marathon runners experience mild hyponatremia during a race. But runners who consume only pure water during a race can develop severe hyponatremia because the drinking water dilutes the sodium in the bloodstream. Such runners may experience neurological disorders as a result of the severe hyponatremia and require emergency treatment.

Chapter Seven
[1] Arthur Drechsler, *The Weightlifting Encyclopedia: A Guide to World Class Performance* (Whitestone, N.Y.: A IS A Communications, 1998), 412.

Chapter Eight
[1] Virgil Carrington Jones, *The Hatfields and the McCoys* (Chapel Hill: The University of North Carolina Press, 1948), 18.
[2] *Ibid.*, 21.
[3] *Ibid.*, 38.
[4] *Ibid.*, 53.
[5] *Ibid.*, 55.
[6] *Ibid.*, 248.
[7] *Ibid.*, 223.
[8] *Ibid.*, 231.
[9] *Ibid.*, 227.
[10] *Ibid.*, 231.
[11] *Ibid.*, 239-240.
[12] *Ibid.*, 240.

Author's Note: The book written by Virgil C. Jones is recognized among historians as the most factual account of the feud.

Documentary validation was very important to the author in presenting the story of the Hatfields and the McCoys.

Chapter Nine
[1]Ed Reese, *The Life and Ministry of Billy Bray (1794-1868)* Christian Hall of Fame Series, No. 38 (Glenwood, Ill.: Fundamental Publishers, 1976), 4.

[2]*Ibid.*, 2.

[3]*Ibid.*, 13.

[4]Arnold Dallimore, *C. H. Spurgeon: The New Biography* (Chicago: Moody Press, 1984), 77.

[5]*Ibid.*, 78.

Chapter Ten
[1]Fiona Marshall and Peter Cheevers, *Positive Options for Seasonal Affective Disorder SAD* (Alameda, Calif.: Hunter House Inc., Publishers, 2003), 4.

[2]*Ibid.*, 14.

[3]*Ibid.*, 104.

*"How to gain, how to keep,
and how to recover happiness is in fact
for most men at all times the secret
motive of all they do."*
                                   –William James

Sources Consulted

American Psychiatric Association. *Diagnostic and Statistical Manual of Mental Disorders, Fourth Edition, Text Revision.* Washington, DC: American Psychiatric Association, 2000.

Bloomfield, Harold H., M.D. and Peter McWilliams. *How to Heal Depression.* Los Angeles: Prelude Press, 1994.

Braun, Stephen. *The Science of Happiness: Unlocking the Mysteries of Mood.* New York: John Wiley & Sons, Inc., 2000.

Cousens, Gabriel, M.D. with Mark Mayell. *Depression-Free for Life.* New York: Harper Collins Publishers, 2000.

Daley, Dennis C., Ph.D. and Howard B. Moss, M.D., *Dual Disorders.* Center City, Minn.: Hazelden, 2002.

Dallimore, Arnold. *C. H. Spurgeon: The New Biography.* Chicago: Moody Press, 1984.

Dean, Melanie A., Ph.D. *Borderline Personality Disorder.* Kansas City: Compact Clinicals, 2001.

Dreschsler, Arthur. *The Weightlifting Encyclopedia: A Guide to*

World Class Performance. Whitestone, N.Y.: AISA Communications, 1998.

Gotlib, Ian H. and Susan A. Nolan, contributing editors. "Depressive Disorders." *Psychopathology in Adulthood.* Second Edition. Boston: Allyn & Bacon, 2000.

Hersen, Michel and Alan S. Bellack. *Psychopathy in Adulthood.* Needham Heights, Mass.: Allyn and Bacon, 2000.

Jamison, Kay Redfield. *An Unquiet Mind.* New York: Vintage Books, 1995.

Jones, Virgil Carrington. *The Hatfields and the McCoys.* Chapel Hill: The University of North Carolina Press, 1948.

Kramlinger, Keith, M.D., Editor in Chief. *Mayo Clinic on Depression.* Rochester, Minn.: Mayo Clinic Health Information, 2001.

Lilly to Add Warning to Strattera Label. Indianapolis. September 29, 2005. http://www.cbsnews.com/stories/2005/09/20/ap/business/main.

Marshall, Fiona and Peter Cheevers. *Positive Options for Seasonal Affective Disorder SAD.* Alameda, Calif.: Hunter House Inc., Publishers, 2003.

Medina, John, Ph.D. *Depression: How It Happens, How It Heals.* n.c.: CME, Inc. and New Harbinger Publications, Inc., 1998.

Moser, Margaret and Bill Crawford. *Rock Stars Do the Dumbest Things.* New York: St. Martin's Books, 1998.

Nardo, Don. *The Battle of Marathon*. San Diego: Lucent Books, 1996.

Paul Ostapuk. "The First Marathon Run: The History of Phidippides." http:///www.lakepowell.net/marathon.html, 11/29/2005.

Preston, Dr. John. *You Can Beat Depression: A Guide to Prevention and Recovery*. Third Edition. Atascadero, Calif.: Impact Publishers, Inc, 2001.

Rapp, Doris, M.D. *Is This Your Child's World?* New York: William Morrow & Co., 1991.

Reese, Ed. *The Life and Ministry of Billy Bray (1794-1868)* Christian Hall of Fame Series. No. 38. Glenwood, Ill.: Fundamental Publishers, 1976.

Sahley, Billie Jay, Ph.D. *The Natural Way to Control Hyperactivity*. San Antonio: Pain & Stress Therapy Center Publications, 1994.

Seer Cancer Statistic Review, 1975-2002: Lifetime Risk (Percent) of Being Diagnosed With Cancer. http://seer.cancer.gov/CSR/1975_2002/results_single/sect_01_table.14.

Wasmer Smith, Linda. *Depression: What It Is, How to Beat It*. Berkeley Heights, N.J.: Enslow Publishers, Inc., 2000.

Winget, Pat and Barbara Kantrowitz. "Young and Depressed." *Newsweek*. Volume CXL. No. 15. 7 Oct. 2002.

Wright, Josephine, M.D. *Do We Really Need Ritalin? A Family Guide to Attention Deficit Hyperactivity Disorder*. New York: Avon Books, 1997.

NOTES